Tasty Bytes

Cookbook

Best-of-the-Internet Vegetarian Recipes

edited by Cynthia Holzapfel

The Book Publishing Company
Summertown, Tennessee

Cover Design: Sheryl Karas
Interior Design: Cynthia Holzapfel, Warren C. Jefferson

Book Publishing Company
P. O. Box 99
Summertown, TN 38483
800-695-2241

ISBN 1-57067-037-4

Tasty Bytes cookbook : best-of-the-Internet vegetarian recipes
    edited by Cynthia Holzapfel.
        p.   cm.
    Includes index.
    ISBN 1-57067-037-4 (alk. paper)
    1. Vegetarian cookery. 2. Vegetarianism--Information services
I. Holzapfel, Cynthia
TX837.T36 1997
641.5'636--dc21   96-46752
                                                              CIP

Calculations for the nutritional analyses in this book are based on the average number of servings listed with the recipes and the average amount of an ingredient, if a range is called for. Calculations are rounded up to the nearest gram. If two options for an ingredient are listed, the first one is used. Not included are optional ingredients, serving suggestions, or fat used for frying, unless the amount of fat is specified in the recipe.

Contents

Preface

My first introduction to the Internet was back in 1994 when it was just becoming a buzz word in the media. Our publishing company began to get a slow but steady flow of inquiries from people who indicated they had heard about us "on the Net." After a while my curiosity was piqued: What were people saying about us and where?

Most discussion about our vegetarian books and products was happening within the newsgroups. The World Wide Web has become the most glamorous aspect of cyberspace, but for many years the newsgroups were, and in many cases still are, the workhorses of the Internet, where people of like interests came together to share information and debate the facts. It was within the two oldest and best known vegetarian newsgroups, rec.food.veg and rec.food.veg.cooking, that I found an on-going discussion, not only of our products, but a myriad of fascinating topics. And recipes. An amazing number of recipes were being shared among participants. As a cookbook editor, I was impressed by the number of original creations available at the stroke of a key. Suddenly it occurred to me there was a cookbook there.

I was delighted at the response to my idea: a cookbook of recipes contributed by people over the Internet. Instead of receiving royalties for their contributions, they would donate their proceeds to a non-profit organization of their choosing related to vegetarian concerns. Recipes poured in and the staff here at Book Publishing had the "hard" work of sampling and critiquing them all. (Needless to say, they miss those delicious tasting sessions.) The results are the the the recipes you'll find in this book.

Many thanks to Bobbi Pasternak who graciously contributed the section on vegetarian information available on the premium services. For many of you, this will be the quickest and easiest way to tap into the wellspring of information out there. I am also grateful to Michelle Dick, owner of FATFREE, The Low-Fat Vegetarian Mailing List, as several recipe contributors came from that connection. A special word of appreciation goes to Bob Bland, Chuck Narad, and Michael Traub. Bob is the king of zesty spices and pasta dishes; Chuck's humor and exuberance for life and good food is infectious; and Michael puts in many hours maintaining the FAQ (frequently asked questions) section of rec.food.veg, the oldest vegetarian newsgroup. Their contributions were generous and delicious.

The number of information sources for vegetarians on the Web is exploding. One site called www.veg.org/veg/ has many resource listings. You can also check newspapers and magazines for addresses of new interest groups, archives of articles, listings of restaurants, and, of course, locations for recipes. It would be difficult for any publication to keep up with this rapidly increasing number of sources, but with the powerful search engines now available to most users, this information is just a few key strokes away. I hope this book will inspire you to explore as many of these possibilites as you can. In the meantime, bon appétit! :-)

Cynthia Holzapfel

What's On The Internet For Vegetarians

Vegetarians active on the commercial online services agree that these services offer one important element that the Internet often does not; they offer a strong sense of community for participating vegetarians. Mel Dillenbeck, a vegetarian for 18 months, says, "I remember how unsure of everything I was in the beginning and how the veggie forum felt like a safety net." Mel is a member of the CompuServe Vegetarian Forum, but her sentiments are echoed by members of America Online's Vegetarians Online, Microsoft's Vegetarian SubForum, and Prodigy's Food Bulletin Board Vegetarian section.

The major commercial online services are America Online (AOL), CompuServe (CIS), Microsoft Network (MSN), and Prodigy. Their pricing and available services vary. All services offer electronic mail (e-mail), message boards, and real-time "chat." E-mail allows subscribers to exchange mail messages with anyone who has an Internet e-mail address, whether or not the addressee is on the same service. Message boards, where members may read and post messages, offer public discussion of a wide variety of top-ics. Real time "chat" allows users to carry on "conversations" with other members who are online at the same time. A feature long available on all services except Prodigy is the file library which allows users to place (upload) or retrieve (download) text files and software. All of the commercial online services offer access to the Internet's USENET news groups and the World Wide Web, but only AOL and MSN have the ability to offer these features from within their vegetarian areas. In deciding which service is right for you, consider how much time you will be online, what features offered by the service you will use, and your comfort level with the service's interface. The best way to determine all of this is to take advantage of the free trial memberships offered by all services. Phone numbers for more information are as follows:

America Online	800-827-6364
CompuServe	800-848-8199
Microsoft Network	800-386-5550
Prodigy	800-776-3449

Each of the "big four" online services has a primary place where vegetarians gather. Some also offer other areas of potential interest to vegetarians. The areas discussed here are available only to members of the particular online service, and can not be accessed from the Internet. AOL "keywords," MSN and CIS "go" words, and Prodigy "jump" words denote the shortcuts used to find the specified area.

America Online

AOL's vegetarian activity is centered in Vegetarians Online, a division of the AOL Cooking Club. To get to there, use AOL Keyword: VEGAN. Vegetarians Online contains the following areas:

* Vegetarianism: Questions & Answers—basic information for beginners
* Vegetarian Dialogue—a message board with a wide variety of topics
* Vegetarian Library—vegetarian files to download
* Vegetarian Book Reviews—reviews of books of interest to vegetarians
* Vegetarian Sites on World Wide Web—quick links to the best veggie web sites
* Vegetarian News groups—easy access to vegetarian USENET news groups
* Vegetarian Recipes—message board of vegetarian and vegan recipes
* Profiles in Curryage—self-introductions and photos of Vegetarians Online members
* Play the Vegetarian Game!—A link to the Vegetarian Resource Group's Vegetarian Game on World Wide Web

An online store offers interactive shopping for vegetarian items. Special features have included sections about The Great American Meatout, World Animal Awareness Week, and Soyfoods. Vegetarians Online also offers advertising and promotional opportunities for vendors offering vegan products.

There are several live weekly chats for vegetarians in the Cooking Club's Cooks Nook conference room. On Sundays at 10:30 P.M. ET, Earth-Friendly Living offers discussion of and practical tips for a cruelty-free and environmentally-friendly lifestyle. Tuesdays

at 9:30 P.M. ET. Vegetarian Teen's Chat invites teens who are vegetarian or are interested in learning more about vegetarianism to
participate in a one-hour discussion. Vegetarian Cooking Basics follows at 10:30 P.M. ET, teaching participants the skills they need to
become comfortable preparing plant-based meals.

Two chats are currently held on Wednesday evenings. Now in
its third year, Vegetarian Living at 9 P.M. ET focuses on food, cooking, health, nutrition, resources, mutual support, and camaraderie.
The chat begins with a scheduled topic, but the floor is open to
topics of the participants' choice later in the hour. At 10 P.M. ET
Vegetarian Issues Chat offers discussion of topics related to the eth-
ical and social aspects of vegetarianism or drawn from media rep-
resentation of vegetarianism and vegetarian issues. A Thursday
night Vegetarian Singles Chat will launch soon. Look for specific
chat topics and additions to the schedule in Vegetarians Online's
Chat Information and Schedule section. To get to the chats, use
Keyword: cookclub, then choose Cooking Chat, then Cooks Nook.

Vegetarians Online offers a monthly e-mail newsletter, VEGUPDATE.
While it is produced by and for AOL members, it includes content
of interest to other vegetarians as well. Subscriptions are open to
anyone with e-mail and may be requested by sending an e-mail
message to:
LISTSERV@LISTSERV.AOL.COM.

The message body should read SUB VEGUPDATE followed by
your first and last names.

Vegetarians Online is hosted and staffed by vegetarians.
Vegetarians Online can be contacted by e-mail at:
nursebobbi@aol.com
or by snail mail at:
PO Box 11841
Burke, VA 22009

The EnviroLink Network on AOL (Keyword: ENVIROLINK)
offers the best environmental news and information available on
any commercial online service. EnviroNews Service (ENS), with
800 reporters worldwide, offers up to the minute coverage of environmental news, including issues in animal rights and vegetarian

health and nutrition. "One World Magazine" explores cultural and biological diversity around our planet. The EnviroLink Library contains information on every environmental topic imaginable. Tree Huggers Grove is a gathering place for activists which offers action alerts from around the world and tools to help activists to communicate effectively with their legislators and the media. EnviroLink on AOL gives members a chance to voice their views and ask their questions through message boards and live chats. EnviroLink plans to assist other environmental non-profit groups who wish to have a presence on AOL.

Elsewhere on AOL, the Pet Care Forum Message Center has a section dedicated to discussion of Animals and Society. In this section, several folders deal with animal rights and animal welfare topics. Find them at Keyword: PETS. In the Jewish Community Online Forum (Keyword: JEWISH), ♣ Jewish Vegetarians folder is available in the Holidays, Celebrations, and Food message board.

CompuServe

Vegetarians on CompuServe gather in the Vegetarian Forum. To visit, use the command "go vegetarian." The forum includes a variety of message and library sections dedicated to vegetarian topics and a conference room for live chats. In addition to the sections dedicated to various vegetarian foods, there are sections titled Nutrition & Health, Vegetarian Children, The New Vegetarian, Outreach & Resources, Lifestyles, Vegetarian Times Magazine, Menus & Planning, and In Print & On Disk. Live conferences are held on a regular basis. Check the forum notices for upcoming events. The company which owns and manages The Vegetarian Forum is non-vegetarian, as are some of the forum staff members.

Other CompuServe areas which may be of interest to vegetarians include the Natural Medicine Forum (go holistic), the Animals Issues section of Animals Forum (go animals), and the Animal Rights section of Earth Forum (go earth). Before deciding to spend time in Earth Forum, members should be aware that the forum's administrator, Joe Reynolds, is former Eastern editor of "Field & Stream" magazine and is now publisher of "Outdoors Network Magazine." Both publications are devoted to sport hunting.

The Microsoft Network

Microsoft Network is available to individuals running Windows95. A Vegetarian SubForum is included in What's Cooking...Online! Forum. The Vegetarian SubForum currently includes the following sections:

* Chatter—general introductions and discussion
* Organizations & Events—Information about international, national, and local groups and events
* Health & Nutrition
* Issues & Information
* Vegetarian Journal—excerpt files of the bi-monthly Vegetarian Journal and the quarterly Foodservice Update, both published by the Vegetarian Resource Group.
* Vegetarian Food & Cooking Discussion
* Vegetarian Recipes, including a sub-folder for recipe conversions
* Vegetarian Society—files from the Vegetarian Society of the United Kingdom

The forum is flexibly structured according to the needs and interests of its membership. On MSN, messages can contain embedded library files or links to other objects or areas on MSN or on the World Wide Web.

Vegetarian Chats are held Tuesday nights at 8 P.M. ET and take place in the What's Cooking Online! chat room. Upcoming chats are posted in the Chatter section of the subforum. To find the Vegetarian SubForum, use the command Go Vegetarian.

MSN recently lauched new software, moving its focus to the World Wide Web. Members using the new MSN software will still have access to the older structure described above by choosing "Classic MSN." However, member participation there is declining as the focus on providing new content is occurring on the Web-based part of the service. To access the vegetarian content on the New MSN, go to URL http://forums.msn.com/cooking or choose these MSN newsgroups:

    msn.forums.cooking.veg.chatter
    msn.forums.cooking.veg.food
    msn.forums.cooking.veg.health
    msn.forums.cooking.veg.issues
    msn.forums.cooking.veg.orgs
    msn.forums.cooking.veg.recipes

What's Cooking Online! Forum Manager Perry Lowell is a long-time vegetarian. Questions about the MSN Vegetarian SubForum may be directed to her by e-mail at:

    Perry_Lowell_FM@msn.com.

Prodigy

Prodigy does not offer a full vegetarian forum, but boasts a friendly and active Vegetarian section on the Food Bulletin Board. (JUMP FOOD BBS) The section is hosted by vegetarian Team Rep Catherine Leslie who sets the tone and provides an abundance of helpful information and tasty recipes.

Vegetarian Chats are held each Saturday at 9 P.M. ET in Common Interests, Member Room, and Vegheads. The Food BBS Archives provide a year's worth of message postings from this active group of vegetarians. Many of the Prodigy vegetarians have met each other in person at national vegetarian events. Cath can be contacted by e-mail at The_Veg_Goddess@prodigy.com. Chris Mitchell, a vegetarian for over 20 years and CompuServe member for 12 years, has enjoyed online communication with vegetarians from the United States, United Kingdom, Germany, Spain, Japan, Canada, South America, Australia, Israel, and South Africa. Chris finds it interesting that the expressed "problems, joys, concerns, sensibilities, and habits of vegetarians world-wide are very similar."

Indeed, a familiar refrain in introductory messages posted on all of the commercial services is, "I'm so glad I've found this place! I thought I was alone." Even if you're the only vegetarian you know in the "real world," there are virtual vegetarian communities waiting to welcome you on America Online, CompuServe, Microsoft Network, and Prodigy.

Bobbi Pasternak, RNC
NurseBobbi@aol.com

Salads

Lara Rice Salad 12

Very Quick & Easy Couscous Salad 13

Black Bean Salad 14

Three Bean Salad 15

Red & Green Slaw 16

Big Greek Salad 17

Hot Potato Salad 18

Bean & Cactus Salad 19

Amaretto Fruit Salad 20

Lara Rice Salad

Yield: 10 to 12 cups

½ cup wild rice
1½ cups brown rice

Tofu "croutons":
1 (3 x 3-inch) block of tofu,
    sliced into ½-inch cubes
Tamari to cover
Cooking oil (safflower and
    sesame are good)

Dressing:
Juice of 1 lemon
2 tablespoons olive oil

1 pear, sliced into bite-size pieces
1 green pepper, sliced into bite-
    size pieces
1 small (6 ounce) jar sliced green
    olives (about 1¼ cups),
    drained
¾ cup toasted sunflower seeds,
    cashews, or any nuts you like
    (optional)

Combine the wild rice and brown rice, and simmer in 4 cups of water until tender and well done. Allow the rice to cool.

Prepare the tofu "croutons" by marinating the tofu in the tamari, then deep frying in oil until brown and puffy. Drain and cool.

To make the dressing, pour the lemon juice into a small jar, add the oil, cover, and shake.

Combine all the ingredients. Serve on a decorative bed of lettuce, and enjoy!

Lara Rice
bs560@freenet.carleton.ca

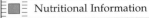 Nutritional Information

Per cup: Calories: 244,
Protein: 7 gm., Fat: 12 gm.,
Carbohydrates: 25 gm.

Very Quick & Easy Couscous Salad

Yield: 4 servings

1½ cups water
1 cup couscous
Juice of 1 lemon
4 to 6 teaspoons salad oil (dark sesame is delicious)
1 medium tomato, chopped into small cubes
1 cup finely chopped parsley or your favorite combination of fresh herbs

Bring the water to a boil in a small saucepan. When the water is boiling, quickly stir in the couscous, cover, and remove from the heat. Let set for 10 minutes.

To make the dressing, pour the lemon juice into a small jar, add the oil, cover, and shake.

After 10 minutes, fluff the couscous by stirring with a wooden spoon. Mix all the ingredients into a salad bowl, and serve.

Lara Rice
bs560@freenet.carleton.ca

Nutritional Information

Per serving: Calories: 178, Protein: 4 gm., Fat: 5 gm., Carbohydrates: 27 gm.

Black Bean Salad

Yield: 6 cups

1½ cups cooked black beans
¾ cup fresh or frozen corn
1 big slice of onion, chopped
½ green bell pepper, chopped
½ red hot pepper, chopped
⅓ teaspoon cumin
¾ cup tomato salsa
1 tablespoon chopped cilantro
A few dashes of cayenne pepper
Freshly ground black pepper to
    taste
Salt to taste

Mix the beans and corn with the rest of the ingredients, and chill. This is best if you let it set for a few hours before eating. Serve on a bed of fresh lettuce with hot tortillas on the side.

Valerie Cashman
vkc@teleport.com

Nutritional Information

Per cup: Calories: 88,
Protein: 4 gm., Fat: 0 gm.,
Carbohydrates: 17 gm.

Three Bean Salad

Yield: approximately 8 cups

Dressing:
¼ cup honey
½ cup vinegar
1 tablespoon olive oil
Freshly ground black pepper to taste
Dash of paprika
¼ teaspoon each: garlic powder, marjoram, and basil

Salad:
1 (16-ounce) can wax beans, drained
1 (16-ounce) can chick-peas, rinsed and drained
1 (16-ounce) can kidney beans, rinsed and drained
1 (16-ounce) can hominy, drained
4 scallions, chopped

In small bowl, whisk together the dressing ingredients. Toss in a large bowl with the salad ingredients. Let stand a couple of hours, tossing occasionally for best flavor.

Ruth J Fink-Winter
wfink@iastate.edu

Nutritional Information

Per cup: Calories 279,
Protein: 10 gm., Fat: 3 gm.,
Carbohydrates: 44 gm.

Red & Green Slaw

Yield: 6 cups

ed.—An unusual combination of ingredients makes this slaw more than memorable.

3 cups shredded red cabbage
3 cups shredded green cabbage
1 small red onion, thinly sliced
2 tablespoons olive oil
2 tablespoons balsamic vinegar
½ cup minced cilantro
½ teaspoon salt
⅛ teaspoon cayenne pepper
2 tablespoons orange juice

Toss all of the ingredients together, and let stand for 30 minutes.

Chuck Narad

 Nutritional Information

Per cup: Calories: 64,
Protein: 1 gm., Fat: 4 gm.,
Carbohydrates: 5 gm.

Big Greek Salad

Yield: 6 servings

This delicious and filling green salad can also be stuffed into whole wheat pita bread halves for fun sandwiches. To make this salad in advance, mix together the dressing ingredients and add to all the other ingredients, except the lettuce, up to a day in advance. Add the lettuce immediately before serving.

2 cucumbers, peeled and sliced
2 tomatoes, cut into wedges
4 scallions, thinly sliced
8 Greek kalamata olives, pitted
   and sliced
⅓ cup crumbled feta cheese

Dressing:
2 tablespoons red wine vinegar
2 tablespoons lemon juice
¼ cup extra-virgin olive oil
2 teaspoons oregano
Salt and white pepper to taste
10 leaves romaine lettuce, torn
   into bite-size chunks
Lemon wedges for garnish

Mix the cucumbers, tomatoes, scallions, olives, and feta cheese in a serving bowl.

In a small mixing bowl, whisk together the vinegar, lemon juice, olive oil, and oregano until smooth. Season to taste with salt and white pepper.

Add the lettuce to the serving bowl, and pour the dressing over the salad. Gently mix until the dressing is evenly distributed.

Serve immediately.

Nanette Blanchard
76702.3406@compuserve.com

 Nutritional Information

Per serving: Calories 150,
Protein: 2 gm., Fat: 12 gm.,
Carbohydrates: 6 gm.

Hot Potato Salad

Yield: 4 to 6 servings

The vinegar, pickle, and spices give this dish the extra flavor it needs as a hot dish. The red waxy potatoes are essential, as they give the dish texture. I grow Red Eriks, Red Golds, Desiree, and the purplish Caribes in my Vermont garden. They all have better flavor at some point in the storage cycle than the supermarket reds, which are usually Red Norlands. The Eriks are no longer commercially available, but are being maintained by the Seed Savers Exchange, a network of true amateur growers based in Decorah, Iowa. They are maintaining our food heritage in the face of governmental and commercial indifference.

8 to 12 red potatoes—the
    smaller the better (2 to 3
    pounds)

1 onion, chopped (about ½ cup)
1 stalk celery, sliced
4 tablespoons dill or sweet
    pickle, thinly sliced, or to taste
1 to 2 tablespoons olive oil
2 tablespoons capers

1 cup water or vegetable stock
½ cup vinegar
1 teaspoon paprika
½ teaspoon mustard seeds
½ teaspoon dry mustard
2 to 3 tablespoons chopped
    parsley or chives

Steam the potatoes until tender, about 15 to 20 minutes. Slice while hot.

Using a 2-quart saucepan, sauté the onion, celery, and pickles in the olive oil. When the onion becomes translucent (about 3 to 5 minutes), add the capers and sauté for 1 more minute.

Add the water or stock, vinegar, paprika, mustard seeds, and dry mustard. Heat to boiling and add the sliced potatoes. Cook until most of the water or stock is absorbed or evaporated, about 3 minutes. Serve with the chopped parsley or chives.

Bob Bland
bland@sover.net
www.sover.net/~bland

 Nutritional Information

Per serving: Calories: 248,
Protein: 3 gm., Fat: 4 gm.,
Carbohydrates: 50 gm.

Bean & Cactus Salad

Yield: 8 to 10 servings

1½ cups cooked garbanzo
    beans, with ¼ cup cooking
    water
1½ cups cooked kidney, black
    turtle, or other beans, plus ¼
    cup cooking water
1½ cups cooked Mexican-style
    cactus (nopalitos), well rinsed
    and chopped into 1½-inch
    pieces
2 tablespoons capers
3 tablespoons balsamic vinegar
2 tablespoons extra-virgin olive
    oil (optional)
¼ cup tamari
3 to 4 cloves fresh garlic, peeled
    and finely chopped

Mix the beans and their cooking waters together. Add the cactus, capers, vinegar, olive oil (if using), and tamari. Stir and taste, adding more cooking water if the mixture is too salty, or more vinegar or tamari if too bland. Stir in the chopped garlic.

Refrigerate in a covered bowl for 24 hours or overnight. If you're not overly fond of garlic, start with a single clove, and refrigerate the salad for several hours. Then add more garlic to taste. Canned beans may be used if you do not choose to cook dried beans. If you are using canned beans and cactus, try to use brands with no preservatives.

William B. Severson
mpmp@best.com

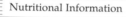 Nutritional Information

Per serving: Calories 113,
Protein: 5 gm., Fat: 0 gm.,
Carbohydrates: 21 gm.

Amaretto Fruit Salad

Yield: 6 servings

2 apples
1 orange
1 banana
1 bunch seedless green grapes
1 large (20-ounce) can pineapple
  chunks
Handful of dried cranberries
1 cup yogurt
3 tablespoons amaretto
1 tablespoon honey

Slice, seed, and peel the fruit as appropriate. Combine them in a bowl; pour the pineapple and juice on top. (The juice keeps everything from turning brown.) Toss, top with the cranberries, and let set overnight.

Mix the yogurt, amaretto, and honey. Serve the fruit salad in small bowls with a dollop of the yogurt mixture on top.

Chuck Narad

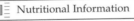 Nutritional Information

Per serving: Calories: 190,
Protein: 3 gm., Fat: 1 gm.,
Carbohydrates: 38 gm.

Spreads, Dips & Sauces

Fifteen-Minute Pasta Sauce

Yield: 4 to 6 servings

Here's the sauce I usually whip up for lasagne, but it works great on its own too. For a little fire, I'll add a tablespoon of Busha Brown's Jerk Sauce, or some cumin, or Hell Sauce (scotch bonnet pepper sauce).

1 medium onion, diced
6 to 10 garlic cloves, peeled, smashed, and minced
1 small green pepper, seeds removed and chopped
1 tablespoon olive oil
2 (15-ounce) cans tomato sauce
Herbs and spices: marjoram, basil, parsley, savory, black pepper, bay leaf, oregano, and nutmeg
½ pound mushrooms, chopped
2 small zucchini, grated coarsely
Red wine to taste
Parmesan cheese (optional)

Sauté the onion, garlic, and pepper in the olive oil until soft, then add the tomato sauce. Add any herbs and spices to taste, the way Grandma cooked ("just enough of each!"). Nutmeg is the secret ingredient in really good tomato sauces—add just a touch. Let simmer on low.

Add the mushrooms and zucchini. Sometimes I'll also drain, rinse, and chop a can of straw mushrooms and add them.

A splash of red wine adds nicely to the flavor; pour the rest into the cook and the helpers. For lacto-vegetarians, add a couple of tablespoons of Parmesan cheese a few minutes before serving.

If you like this sauce thicker, add a 6-ounce can of tomato paste.

Chuck Narad

 Nutritional Information

Per serving: Calories: 95,
Protein: 3 gm., Fat: 1 gm.,
Carbohydrates: 18 gm.

Summer-All-The-Time Spread

Yield: about 3 to 3½ cups

Summer-All-The-Time Spread is light, complex, happy in taste, and very adaptable. Use as a sandwich spread or a dip for veggies or chips. If you have a food processor, this is a very quick recipe.

2 cloves garlic, minced or pressed
2 to 3 carrots, shredded
1 pound tofu, mashed
3 to 4 tablespoons tahini
1 tablespoon grated fresh gingerroot
Juice of 1 lemon
½ tablespoon Dijon mustard
½ tablespoon tamari
1 teaspoon powdered cumin, or more to taste
½ teaspoon chili powder, or more to taste
Salt and pepper to taste
2 tablespoons chopped fresh parsley
2 scallions, chopped or diced

If you are using a food processor, first chop the garlic until fine, then replace the chopping blade with the shredder, and shred the carrots. Carefully put the chopping blade back in, and add the tofu and tahini. Blend for about ½ minute. Add the gingerroot, lemon juice, mustard, tamari, cumin, chili powder, salt, and pepper, and blend together. If the consistency is too chunky, drizzle in water as needed to produce a spreadable consistency (like that of hummus). Season to taste and stir in or briefly whip in the parsley and scallions.

If you are working by hand, have all the ingredients prepared. First, mash the tahini and liquid ingredients into the tofu until you are satisfied with the consistency. A little water may be required. Blend in the garlic, ginger, and spices. Finally, stir in the carrots, parsley, and scallions until well mixed.

Janet Ingraham
jingraha@freenet.columbus.oh.us

 Nutritional Information

Per ¼ cup: Calories: 61, Protein: 3 gm., Fat: 4 gm., Carbohydrates: 4 gm.

Pesto

Yield: 2 to 4 servings

There are probably six billion recipes for pesto on this small planet. I favor the traditional pine nuts, but they can run up as high as $16 a pound at my local coop. At that price, I find almonds just as wonderful. In the summer, when I interplant basil with tomatoes, I crop the basil, make gobs of pesto using several nut bases, and freeze it for a quick winter treat. When the tomatoes are ripe, I often chop a few of my ultra-sweet Chelseas and add them to the pesto.

½ cup Parmesan cheese
2 to 3 cloves garlic, roughly
   chopped
⅓ cup pine nuts, as available, or
   blanched slivered almonds
2 cups packed fresh basil or
   tarragon
Extra-virgin olive oil, as needed

In a food processor, process the Parmesan until almost dusty, and remove to a bowl. Process the garlic until minced, and remove to a bowl. Process the pine nuts until well chopped, and remove to a bowl. Finally, process the basil until chopped or shredded (may require scraping from the sides of the processor bowl). Mix the ingredients in the bowl well with a fork. Gradually add the olive oil until the ingredients adhere, but the oil does not overwhelm the mix. A change in sound and texture occurs when the mix is "right." If you add too much oil the pesto is okay, but the fat content is higher than it should be.

This is wonderful with a light fresh pasta, such as capellini or linguini. Lightly oil the pasta, then toss with pesto.

Bob Bland
bland@sover.net
www.sover.net/~bland

Nutritional Information

Per serving: Calories: 298,
Protein: 14 gm., Fat: 20 gm.,
Carbohydrates: 16 gm.

24

Sautéed Veggie Purée

Yield: 6 servings

A mixed vegetable sauté goes into the blender to make a delicious pasta sauce, sandwich filling, topping for fried tofu, or snack by the spoonful.

2 tablespoons olive oil for sautéing
1 large onion, coarsely chopped
3 medium carrots, coarsely chopped
3 stalks celery, coarsely chopped
1 very large or 2 small bell peppers, coarsely chopped
2 cloves garlic, minced
Dash of sesame oil
2 Vegex cubes (or other vegetable bouillon cubes or powder), dissolved in ¼ cup hot water
2 tablespoons tamari
2 tablespoons red wine vinegar
Salt and freshly ground black pepper to taste

Heat a wok or large saucepan over medium-high heat, and add the olive oil. Sauté the onions for a few minutes until soft. Add the carrots and celery, and sauté about 5 more minutes. Add the bell peppers and garlic, and sauté for several more minutes. When all the vegetables are done, reduce the heat.

Whisk together the sesame oil, vegetable bouillon cubes, tamari, and vinegar, and carefully add to the sauté. Season to taste with salt and black pepper, and remove from the heat.

When the mixture cools a little, transfer it to a blender and purée. Serve hot, cold, or at room temperature.

Janet Ingraham
jingraha@freenet.columbus.oh.us

 Nutritional Information

Per serving: Calories: 76,
Protein: 1 gm., Fat: 4 gm.,
Carbohydrates: 7 gm.

Vegetable-Topped Hummus

Yield: 8 servings

Tahini is also called sesame paste and can be found in health food stores, Middle Eastern markets, and in some supermarkets.

1 (16-ounce) can garbanzo
   beans, drained
2 tablespoons tahini
2 tablespoons lemon juice
1 clove garlic, peeled
¼ teaspoon salt
1 tomato, finely chopped
2 tablespoons parsley
2 green onions, finely chopped

In a food processor or blender, process the garbanzo beans, tahini, lemon juice, garlic, and salt until smooth. Scoop out into a serving bowl. In a small mixing bowl, combine the tomato, parsley, and green onions. Arrange the tomato mixture on top of the bean mixture. Serve with wedges of pita bread or assorted crackers.

Nanette Blanchard
76702.3406@compuserve.com

 Nutritional Information

Per serving: Calories: 122,
Protein: 5 gm., Fat: 2 gm.,
Carbohydrates: 18 gm.

Overnight Mushroom Pâté

Yield: about 3 cups

8 ounces mushrooms, sliced
1 onion, chopped
2 tablespoons butter or
   margarine
2 tablespoons soy sauce
1½ teaspoons ground cumin
1 tablespoon chopped fresh sage
Salt and freshly ground black
   pepper to taste

Sauté the mushrooms and onion in the butter or margarine over low heat for about 10 minutes, or until the mushrooms release their juices. Add the remaining ingredients and purée in a food processor until finely chopped. Place in a serving dish, cover, and refrigerate overnight before serving. Bring to room temperature before serving.

Nanette Blanchard
76702.3406@compuserve.com

 Nutritional Information

Per ¼ cup: Calories: 29,
Protein: 1 gm., Fat: 2 gm.,
Carbohydrates: 2 gm.

Melon Salsa

Yield: 3 cups (good appetizer for 4 to 6 people)

Salsa has, thankfully, passed ketchup in sales. This recipe combines the "original" ketchup, the Indonesian soy sauce called "ketjap" (if available) with melon in a wild salsa combo.

¼ cup dry-roasted peanuts
3 cloves garlic, roughly chopped
¼ cup sweet soy sauce, such as the Indonesian ketjap mantis or standard good quality soy sauce and a teaspoon of sugar or honey
Grated rind of 1 lime
Juice of 1 lime
1 jalapeño, minced
½ cup fresh cilantro, stems removed and roughly chopped
½ cup fresh parsley, stems removed and roughly chopped
1 melon, such as cantaloupe or honeydew

Place the peanuts in a food processor, and pulse 2 or 3 times until very roughly chopped. Add the garlic and pulse again 5 to 10 times until the garlic is minced and the peanuts are in small pieces. Add the soy sauce, lime rind, lime juice, jalapeño, cilantro, and parsley, and process briefly. Remove the seeds and rind, chop the melon into 1-inch cubes, and place in a bowl. Pour the peanut mixture over the melon, and toss. Cover and refrigerate for at least 1 hour. This salsa can stored for three days.

Bob Bland
bland@sover.net
www.sover.net/~bland

Nutritional Information
Per serving: Calories: 101, Protein: 4 gm., Fat: 6 gm., Carbohydrates: 13 gm.

Soups & Stews

Fat-Free No-Cream Asparagus Soup 30

Creamy Brussels Sprout Soup 31

Potato, Carrot, & Leek Soup 32

Curried Potato & Pea Soup 33

Portuguese Tomato Soup 34

Yellow Split Pea Soup 35

White Bean Soup with Feta Cheese 36

Barley-Mushroom Winter Borscht 37

Chilli 38

Mexican Hot Pot 39

Gazpacho 40

Pasta E Fagioli 41

Fat-Free No-Cream Asparagus Soup

Yield: about 8 cups

2 medium onions, chopped (about 2 cups)
2 medium leeks (white and pale green part only), chopped (about 2 cups)
6 cups vegetable stock or broth
2 pounds asparagus, cut into 4-inch pieces
White pepper to taste
1 (12-ounce) package Butter Buds or other imitation butter flavoring (optional)

Microwave the onions and leeks until tender, about 3 minutes on high, or sauté in water over medium heat until tender, about 10 minutes. Add the stock and asparagus to a large saucepan, and simmer until tender, about 15 to 20 minutes. Purée the soup in a blender in batches, and strain through a fine strainer. Return to a clean pot, and season with white pepper to taste. If a butter taste is desired, add the Butter Buds now. This can be served hot or cold with garlic croutons. It keeps well in the refrigerator for several days.

Variations:

You can replace the asparagus with equal volumes of beets, broccoli, carrots, acorn squash, butternut squash, mushrooms, or red kuri squash. Adjust the simmering time to ensure the vegetables are tender.

Serving Suggestion:

You can make quite an impression by making two different soups at the same time, such as the acorn and butternut squash soups, and serving them in the same bowl. Just slowly pour both soups into opposite sides of the bowl at the same time.

Joe McKay
MCKAY_J@A1.EOP.GOV

 Nutritional Information

Per cup: Calories: 60, Protein: 3 gm., Fat: 0 gm., Carbohydrates: 11 gm.

Creamy Brussels Sprout Soup

Yield: 8 servings

As the new produce buyer for my coop, I sometimes make mistakes. When I ordered way too many brussels sprouts, I felt I should take home at least three pounds myself. Now what to do. Someone mentioned trying a cream of brussels sprout soup recipe. As I don't have one myself, so I made one up.

- 1 tablespoon olive oil
- 1 tablespoon butter (optional—it only provides a buttery flavor)
- 1 cup chopped onions
- 1 tablespoon garlic powder
- 1 cup vegetable broth
- 5 cups potatoes, washed and cut into ½-inch cubes
- 2 cups carrots, washed, peeled, and cut into ½-inch chunks
- 1 tablespoon thyme
- 4 cups water
- 3 tablespoons arrowroot or cornstarch to thicken
- ½ cup water
- 2 pounds fresh brussels sprouts, bottoms trimmed and cut in quarters
- 1 teaspoon salt
- ¼ teaspoon pepper

Heat the olive oil and butter (if using) in a 4-quart stock pan. Add the onions and garlic powder, and sauté. When they are translucent, add the vegetable broth. If the onions start to burn, add another ½ cup of vegetable broth right away. This recipe can be made fat-free by omitting the butter and olive oil and steam-frying the onion and garlic in vegetable broth.

Add the potatoes, carrots, thyme, and 4 cups of water to the onions, and simmer until the potatoes are quite soft, about 20 minutes. Remove about 1 cup of the potatoes and carrots from the soup and about ½ cup of liquid. Purée in a blender or food processor or mash with a potato masher, and mix up thoroughly. Pour the purée back into the soup.

Add the arrowroot to the ½ cup of water, and stir until dissolved. Add to the soup and stir.

Add the brussels sprouts, salt, and pepper to the soup, and simmer until the brussels sprouts are just barely cooked, about 10 minutes.

By this time the purée and cornstarch should have thickened the soup to a creamy consistency. This makes a very tasty, sweet, chunky soup that tastes great with a whole grain roll or a pumpernickel bagel.

Casey Scalzi

Nutritional Information
Per serving: Calories: 173, Protein: 3 gm., Fat: 1 gm., Carbohydrates: 35 gm.

Potato, Carrot & Leek Soup

Yield: 4 to 6 servings

1 pound leeks, well washed and chopped
3 tablespoons vegan margarine
1 tablespoon vegetable oil
4 medium potatoes, cubed (1 to 1½ pounds)
About ¾ pound carrots, cut into ½-inch rounds (2½ cups)
4 cups water
1 teaspoon dried sage, or a few leaves of fresh sage
1 teaspoon soy sauce, or 1 cube vegetable stock (optional)
Salt and freshly ground pepper to taste
1 cup soya milk

Sauté the leeks in the margarine and oil. Add the potatoes and carrots, and stir well. Add the water, sage, and soy sauce or stock, if using, and simmer for about 20 minutes. Add salt and pepper to taste. Blend completely in two batches in a blender or food processor, and return to the pot. Add the soya milk and bring back up to heat.

If you want to be trendy, leave out the carrots, use a little less potato, chill this dish, and call it vichyssoise!

Michael Traub
traub@mistral.co.uk

Nutritional Information
Per serving: Calories: 284, Protein: 4 gm., Fat: 10 gm., Carbohydrates: 43 gm.

Curried Potato & Pea Soup

Yield: 4 servings

One night, I had a cold and wanted a soup that would clear my sinuses. I had potatoes and peas and thought of a sinus-clearing somoza recipe. It wasn't translatable, but I remembered a Tibetan potato soup I once tried. It turned out to provide a good base upon which to create this soup.

1 tablespoon minced gingerroot
1 clove garlic, minced
1 small red onion, chopped
   (about ⅓ cup)
1 tablespoon olive oil
½ teaspoon turmeric
½ teaspoon ground chili
½ teaspoon garam masala*
2 cups diced yellow potatoes
2 cups vegetable stock or water
1 cup peas
1½ teaspoons white vinegar
1 tablespoon soy sauce
Dash black pepper
2 scallions, chopped
¼ cup chopped, fresh cilantro, or
   1 tablespoon dried

Sauté the ginger, garlic, and onion in the olive oil for 1 minute. Add the turmeric, ground chili, and garam masala. Sauté for 1 more minute. Add the potatoes and mix. Cook and stir 1 minute. Add the stock, cover, and cook over low heat for 15 to 20 minutes until the potatoes are tender. Add the peas, vinegar, soy sauce, and black pepper. Simmer 5 more minutes. If the soup is too thick, add more water or stock. Add the scallions and cilantro, and mix well.

Bob Bland
bland@sover.net
www.sover.net/~bland

*Garam masala is a blend of cardamon, cloves, cinnamon, cumin, black pepper, and nutmeg. Dashes of any or all of those spices may be substituted.

Nutritional Information

Per serving: Calories: 141, Protein: 3 gm., Fat: 2 gm., Carbohydrates: 24 gm.

Portuguese Tomato Soup

Yield: 4 servings

2 onions, chopped (about 1 cup)
1 to 2 teaspoons olive oil
1 pint canned tomatoes, or 2 to
   3 cups chopped fresh
   tomatoes
1 cup water or vegetable stock
½ teaspoon black pepper
1 teaspoon or more basil
1 teaspoon thyme
1 bay leaf
2 whole cloves
1 cup diced carrots
Blanched, slivered almonds
   (optional)

Sauté the onions in the olive oil over medium-high heat until browned, about 5 minutes. Add the tomatoes, water or stock, black pepper, basil, thyme, bay leaf, and cloves. Add the carrots, cover, and simmer for 20 minutes until the carrots are tender. Sprinkle with the almonds, if desired.

Bob Bland
bland@sover.net
www.sover.net/~bland

 Nutritional Information

Per serving: Calories: 66,
Protein: 2 gm., Fat: 1 gm.,
Carbohydrates: 11 gm.

Yellow Split Pea Soup

Yield: 8 servings

2 cups dried yellow split peas
1 fresh hot chili pepper (any color)
1 onion, chopped
2 tablespoons extra-virgin olive oil
8 cups water
1 carrot, chopped
1 bunch parsley, chopped
½ bell pepper (any color), chopped
¼ teaspoon dried oregano or thyme
1 bay leaf
1½ teaspoons salt, or to taste
Freshly ground black pepper
½ cup uncooked brown rice (optional)

Rinse the peas well and drain.

Carefully remove the stem and seeds from the hot pepper, and chop. Reserve some of the seeds to flavor the soup, if desired.

In a large soup pot, sauté the onion in the olive oil until soft. Add the hot pepper, split peas, water, carrot, parsley, bell pepper, oregano or thyme, bay leaf, hot pepper seeds (if using), salt, and pepper to taste. Simmer the soup about 2 hours until the peas are soft.

If desired, rice may be added to the soup 40 minutes before the cooking is finished.

Karen Mintzias
km@salata.com

 Nutritional Information

Per serving: Calories: 188, Protein: 9 gm., Fat: 4 gm., Carbohydrates: 29 gm.

White Bean Soup with Feta Cheese

Yield: 6 servings

This recipe is my family's favorite.

- 1 tablespoon olive oil
- ½ cup chopped onions
- 1 teaspoon minced garlic
- 1 cup sliced carrots
- 4 cups cooked white beans, drained, or 2 (15-ounce) cans white beans, rinsed and drained
- 5 cups vegetable broth
- 1 (4-ounce) can chopped green chilies
- ½ teaspoon oregano
- ¼ teaspoon pepper
- 2 cups cabbage, cup into bite-size pieces
- ¼ cup crumbled feta cheese

Heat the oil in a Dutch oven on medium-high heat. Add the onions, garlic, and carrots, and cook, stirring occasionally, until the onions are tender (approximately 5 minutes). Add the beans, broth, chilies (undrained), oregano, and pepper. Bring to a boil, reduce the heat, and simmer approximately 10 minutes. Add the cabbage, cover, and cook about 5 minutes. Serve hot topped with the feta cheese.

Diana Kremenliff
diana_kremenliff@macgate.csuchico.edu

 Nutritional Information

Per serving: Calories: 238,
Protein: 11 gm., Fat: 5 gm.,
Carbohydrates: 38 gm.

Barley-Mushroom Winter Borscht

Yield: 8 to 10 servings

3 cloves garlic, minced
1 large onion, chopped
1 tablespoon olive oil
1 cup barley
½ cup each: baby lima beans, split peas, and brown lentils
7 cups water
5 to 6 small turnips, peeled and cubed (or 2 parsnips or potatoes)
2 carrots, sliced about ½ inch thick
½ to ¾ pound mushrooms, sliced
½ teaspoon pepper, or to taste
2 teaspoons marjoram
1 teaspoon rosemary
⅓ cup tamari
3 tablespoons unsalted butter or margarine (optional)
2 tablespoons miso

Sauté the garlic and onion in the olive oil on medium heat until the onion is translucent. Combine the barley, lima beans, split peas, lentils, and water with the onion and garlic, and bring to a boil. Add the turnips and carrots, reduce the heat to medium-low, and simmer for about 1½ hours, stirring occasionally.

Add the mushrooms, spices, and tamari, and continue cooking over low heat for another hour. Turn off the heat, add the butter or margarine and miso, let set for a few minutes, stir, and serve. ("But grandma, where did they get miso in the Ukraine?" "Shut up and eat your soup.") If cooking the night before, you might want to add 1 cup of water and heat again just before serving. The barley tends to absorb water, and if you omit this extra water, you end up with a tasty gruel.

The butter can be omitted, but it makes for a heartier soup.

Chuck Narad

 Nutritional Information

Per serving: Calories: 180, Protein: 8 gm., Fat: 1 gm., Carbohydrates: 32 gm.

Chilli

Yield: 6 to 8 servings

My first rule in making a good chilli is to not use any chilli powder! I use fresh chillies, and if I find the dish isn't hot enough (extremely rare), then I use a dash of cayenne pepper to bring it up to heat. The main ground spice I use is cumin. I find that is what brings out the flavour of a chilli.

1 large onion, chopped
3 cloves garlic, chopped
2 green chillies, finely chopped
1 red chilli, finely chopped
3 teaspoons cumin
1 teaspoon coriander
1 teaspoon salt
1 tablespoon olive oil
1 tablespoon corn oil

Vegetable version:
1 pound mushrooms
2 medium zucchini (courgettes), chopped
1 red bell pepper (capsicum), chopped
1 green bell pepper (capsicum), chopped
1 yellow bell pepper (capsicum), chopped
1 teaspoon oregano
1 (28-ounce) can tomatoes
1 (15-ounce) can sweet corn, or 1¾ cup frozen corn
1 (15-ounce) can kidney beans, or 1⅔ cups cooked beans
1 (6-ounce) can tomato paste

"Meaty" version:
1½ cups textured vegetable protein
1¼ cups hot water

Marinade:
2 tablespoons olive oil
1 teaspoon oregano
1 teaspoon black pepper
1 vegetable stock cube

Fry the onion, garlic, green and red chillies, cumin, coriander, and salt in the oil, taking care not to burn them.

For the vegetable version, add the mushrooms, zucchini, bell peppers, and oregano.

Add the tomatoes, sweet corn, kidney beans, and tomato paste. Simmer for 45 minutes. Serve the chilli on its own or with rice, or thicken with more tomato purée, and serve stuffed in taco shells, topped with slices of tomatoes and shredded lettuce.

For meaty version, combine the textured vegetable protein and hot water, and let set for 10 minutes. Add the marinade and let set at least 3 hours. Add the marinated textured vegetable protein to the chilli after adding the spices.

Michael Traub
traub@mistral.co.uk

Nutritional Information

Per serving, vegetable version: Calories: 229, Protein: 9 gm., Fat: 5 gm., Carbohydrates: 38 gm.

Per serving, "meaty" version: Calories: 319, Protein: 17 gm., Fat: 8 gm., Carbohydrates: 43 gm.

Mexican Hot Pot

Yield: 6 servings

This colorful vegetarian stew is topped with shredded lettuce.

1 onion, sliced
3 cloves garlic, minced
1 tablespoon canola oil
2 teaspoons crushed red pepper flakes
2 teaspoons dried oregano
1 teaspoon ground cumin
1 (28-ounce) can chopped tomatoes
1 (15-ounce) can garbanzo beans, drained
1 (15-ounce) can pinto beans, drained
2 cups corn kernels, fresh or frozen
1 cup water
6 cups shredded iceberg lettuce

Sauté the onion and garlic in the canola oil in a stock pot for 5 minutes, stirring occasionally. Add the crushed red pepper flakes, oregano, and cumin, and stir well. Stir in the tomatoes, garbanzo beans, pinto beans, corn, and water. Bring to a boil. Reduce the heat, cover, and simmer over medium-low heat for 15 minutes. Top each serving with 1 cup of shredded lettuce. Serve hot.

Nanette Blanchard
76702.3406@compuserve.com

 Nutritional Information

Per serving: Calories: 322,
Protein: 13 gm., Fat: 4 gm.,
Carbohydrates: 57 gm.

Gazpacho

Yield: 6 to 8 servings

3 large tomatoes, skins removed
3 large tomatoes, chopped
1 cucumber
1 green bell pepper
1 small onion
2 cloves garlic
⅓ cup olive oil
⅓ cup wine vinegar
1½ tablespoons lemon juice
1 teaspoon dill
Salt and pepper to taste

Remove the skins from 3 tomatoes by dropping them in boiling water for 30 seconds, then plunging them in cold water. Place the peeled tomatoes, ½ of the cucumber, ½ of the green bell pepper, the onion, garlic, olive oil, vinegar, lemon juice, and dill in a blender, and blend until smooth. Finely chop the 3 remaining tomatoes, remaining ½ cucumber and green bell pepper, and add to the soup. Add the salt and pepper. Chill for at least two hours before serving.

Michael Traub
traub@mistral.co.uk

 Nutritional Information

Per serving: Calories: 125,
Protein: 1 gm., Fat: 9 gm.,
Carbohydrates: 8 gm.

Pasta E Fagioli

Yield: 10 servings

Here is an unusual version of the traditional Venetian bean and macaroni soup. This version includes sun-dried tomatoes and zucchini.

1 onion, chopped
2 tablespoons olive oil
3 cloves garlic, minced
2 zucchini, thinly sliced
2 tablespoons crushed, dried jalapeño peppers
6 sun-dried tomatoes, marinated in oil, drained, and chopped
4 cups cooked and drained cannellini beans
3 cups cooked macaroni
4 cups homemade vegetable broth
2 teaspoons dried oregano
Salt and freshly ground black pepper to taste
Grated Parmesan and extra-virgin olive oil for serving

Sauté the onion in the olive oil for several minutes or until soft. Add the garlic and zucchini, and continue cooking, stirring occasionally, until the zucchini is tender. Add the hot peppers and tomatoes, and sauté an additional 3 minutes. Stir in the beans, macaroni, broth, oregano, and season to taste with salt and black pepper. Cover and simmer over medium heat for 15 minutes. Garnish each bowl with grated Parmesan and a drizzle of some good extra-virgin olive oil if desired.

Nanette Blanchard
76702.3406@compuserve.com

 Nutritional Information

Per serving: Calories: 202,
Protein: 8 gm., Fat: 4 gm.,
Carbohydrates: 34 gm.

Main Dishes

Pastitsio

Yield: 4 to 6 servings

This is a classic Greek dish, and I am sure there are many variations. This is one that I have shaped over the years. It is a good break from my usual tendency toward heat and intense spicyness.

10 to 12 ounces macaroni or
    other tubular pasta
1 cup lentils
1 onion, chopped (about ½ cup)
1 carrot, chopped or grated
    (about ½ cup)
1 to 2 cloves garlic, minced
1 tablespoon soy sauce
¼ teaspoon rosemary
1½ cups water
1½ cups cottage cheese (about
    1 pound)
⅓ cup whole wheat flour
Parmesan to taste
1 cup milk
¼ teaspoon grated nutmeg
¼ teaspoon cinnamon
1 cup bread crumbs for topping

Cook the pasta and set aside.

Cook the lentils with half the onion, the carrot, garlic, soy sauce, rosemary, and water for about 20 to 35 minutes, occasionally checking the liquid, until the lentils are just softened.

In a bowl, combine the cottage cheese and flour. Add the rest of the onion, a grating of Parmesan, the milk, nutmeg, and cinnamon.

Preheat the oven to 350°F.

Layer the pasta, lentils, and cheese mixture in a 2-quart casserole dish. Sprinkle on the bread crumbs for a crusty texture. Bake for 35 minutes or until browned.

Bob Bland
bland@sover.net
www.sover.net/~bland

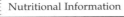

Nutritional Information

Per serving: Calories: 385,
Protein: 23 gm., Fat: 6 gm.,
Carbohydrates: 59 gm.

Pasta Innamorata

Yield: Serves 2 to 4

"Pasta in love," so called since the flavor of it induces a soft, gentle smile of pleasure and appreciation. Using flower honey in this recipe gives a wonderful aroma and taste. Enjoy!

10 ounces penne pasta
2 tablespoons olive oil
3 cloves garlic
1 teaspoon oregano
1 teaspoon parsley
1 teaspoon basil
1 teaspoon chili powder
9 ounces sliced or whole black
   pitted olives
1 pound tomatoes, chopped
2 tablespoons honey
2 tablespoons sweet wine
½ cup heavy cream
Grated Parmesan cheese

Cook the penne as per instructions on the package.

Heat the oil in a saucepan, add the garlic, and fry until it turns a golden yellow. Add the oregano, parsley, basil, chili powder, and olives, and fry for ½ minute.

Add the chopped tomatoes and simmer for 20 to 25 minutes, or until the desired thickness is reached.

Add the honey and wine, and stir for 1 minute. Finally, slowly stir in the cream. Add salt to taste. Pour the sauce over the pasta, and serve immediately. Garnish with freshly grated Parmesan cheese.

Arshiya Noorani

 Nutritional Information

Per serving: Calories: 569,
Protein: 7 gm., Fat: 40 gm.,
Carbohydrates: 44 gm.

Textured Vegetable Protein Spaghetti Sauce

Yield: 4 to 6 servings

1 cup textured vegetable protein granules
1 teaspoon dried oregano
1 teaspoon dried rosemary
1 teaspoon dried basil
1 teaspoon salt
¼ teaspoon black pepper
1 teaspoon vegetable stock, or 1 cube

Sauce:
3 cloves garlic, minced
1 large Spanish onion, chopped
¼ cup olive oil
2 medium zucchini (courgettes), diced
¼ pound mushrooms (optional), sliced
1 (14-ounce) can chopped tomatoes, or 3 large fresh tomatoes, peeled and chopped
½ cup red wine or water
2 teaspoons oregano
1 teaspoon rosemary
½ teaspoon basil
½ teaspoon parsley
tomato purée to thicken

Rehydrate the textured vegetable protein by combining with ⅞ cup boiling water, then add the oregano, rosemary, basil, salt, black pepper, and vegetable stock. Set aside for at least ½ hour (up to 3 hours if possible).

For the sauce, sauté the garlic and onion in the olive oil until tender. Add the textured vegetable protein mixture, and sauté over low heat for about ten minutes. Pour off any unabsorbed liquid. (It's best if this mixture is fairly dry before using.)

Add the zucchini and mushrooms, and continue sautéing until tender. A little extra olive oil may be needed at this time, unless you are using a good nonstick skillet. Because the textured vegetable protein is almost fat-free, the addition of a bit of extra oil here will not make the fat content appreciably higher.

Add the tomatoes, wine, and additional herbs. Cover and simmer for about 20 to 25 minutes. If the sauce is still too runny, add a little tomato purée to thicken. For best results, take the sauce off the heat for a few hours to absorb the flavours. Simmer gently just before serving. Serve over whole wheat spaghetti.

Michael Traub
traub@mistral.co.uk

 Nutritional Information

Per serving: Calories: 198, Protein: 9 gm., Fat: 10 gm., Carbohydrates: 12 gm.

Killer Lasagne

Yield: 6 to 8 servings

I don't use recipes much, but this is the general flow for making a killer veggie lasagne (last time I made it, it killed four guests). There is a recipe for Killer Garlic Bread on page 123.

1 recipe Fifteen-Minute Pasta
Sauce, pg. 22

½ (15-ounce) container low-fat
ricotta cheese
½ pound low-fat cottage cheese
Grated Parmesan

½ pound lasagne noodles,
uncooked
½ pound low-fat mozzarella,
thinly sliced
½ pound Monterey Jack, thinly
sliced
1 medium or 2 small zucchini,
thinly sliced lengthwise
1 (10-ounce) package frozen
chopped spinach

First, prepare the Fifteen-Minute Pasta Sauce, without adding the optional Parmesan cheese.

Preheat the oven to 400°F. Defrost the spinach in the micro wave, and squeeze out all the excess water. In a bowl, mix the spinach, ricotta, and cottage cheese.

Cover the bottom of a 9 x 13-inch baking pan with a thin layer of the sauce. Add a layer of (uncooked!) noodles. Cover with a layer of half the cheese/spinach mixture, a layer of zucchini, and a layer of mozzarella cheese. Sprinkle with Parmesan. Add another layer of sauce, then noodles, then the rest of the cheese/spinach mixture, then zucchini, then the Monterey Jack cheese. Sprinkle on more Parmesan, then another layer of noodles, the last of the sauce, more Parmesan, and a couple of decorative slices of cheese. (If the sauce starts to run low, just pour another can of tomato sauce into the sauce pot midway.) Cover with foil. Bake for 30 minutes, remove the foil, and bake another 10 minutes. Let cool for ten minutes, slice, and serve!

Chuck Narad

Nutritional Information

Per serving: Calories: 433,
Protein: 33 gm., Fat: 20 gm.,
Carbohydrates: 29 gm.

Roasted Eggplant & Pepper-Tomato Sauce Over Pasta

Yield: 4 to 6 servings

1 large eggplant
1 (16-ounce) can tomato sauce
1 (6-ounce) can tomato paste
2 to 4 cloves garlic, pressed
½ yellow onion, chopped
½ red onion, finely chopped (optional)
½ green bell pepper, finely chopped (optional)
2 stalks celery, finely chopped (optional)
1 teaspoon dried oregano, or 1½ teaspoons fresh oregano
1 teaspoon dried basil, or 1½ teaspoons fresh basil
½ teaspoon dried rosemary, or 1½ teaspoons fresh rosemary
¼ teaspoon celery seed
½ teaspoon salt, or to taste
Freshly ground black pepper to taste
¼ teaspoon crushed red pepper (optional)
1 red, yellow, or green bell pepper

Preheat the oven to 450°F.

Wash the unpeeled eggplant and poke it in several places with a knife, making 5 to 6 slits. Place it on a baking pan, and roast in the oven for about 45 minutes. Rotate the eggplant every 10 minutes to help it roast evenly. It will be done when it sags softly and the skin is wrinkled.

While the eggplant is roasting combine the tomato sauce and tomato paste in a saucepan. Bring to a simmer over medium heat, then reduce the heat to medium-low. Add the garlic, onion, celery seed, salt, pepper, and optional ingredients, and simmer for about 10 minutes, stirring occasionally. Then add the oregano, basil, and rosemary, and simmer over very low heat while preparing the pepper and roasted eggplant.

While the sauce is simmering, roast the bell pepper. This works best on a charcoal grill, but you can get good results with a gas range. Place the pepper in the center of a burner, and turn the burner on. Scorch the skin until the pepper is black all over, turning the pepper periodically with a pair of tongs. This should take about 2 minutes. (If you have an electric range, try putting a wire rack just above the heating coil, and place the pepper on the rack, turning the

 Nutritional Information

Per serving: Calories: 112,
Protein: 3 gm., Fat: 0 gm.,
Carbohydrates: 24 gm.

pepper as it blackens.) When the pepper is charred, place it in a paper bag, close the bag, and let it set for about 7 minutes, to allow the smoky flavor to permeate the pepper. Then remove the pepper from the bag, and rinse it under cold running water; the skin will come right off. Cut the pepper into strips 1½ inches long by ¼ inch wide, and stir into the simmering tomato sauce.

Remove the eggplant from the oven, and let it cool slightly for 3 or 4 minutes until you can ginger-ly handle it.

Cut the stem off and you should easily be able to peel the skin off with your fingers (be careful not to burn your hands).

The eggplant should be soft enough so that you can easily make a paste out of it by using a knife to cut it into big chunks. (If it isn't this soft, just cut it into ½-inch cubes.)

Stir the eggplant into the sauce. If you like it hot, in addition to the crushed red pepper, you can also add a vinegar-based hot sauce (like Tabasco). Let the sauce simmer for 2 more minutes, and remove it from the heat. Serve over your favorite freshly cooked pasta.

Dilip Barman
barman@cs.unc.edu
www.cs.unc.edu/~barman/vegetarian.html

Jane's Chili Pasta

Yield: 4 to 6 servings

2 medium onions, chopped
8 mild green chilies, seeded and sliced
2 tablespoons olive oil
1 (28-ounce) can chopped tomatoes
1 pound firm brown mushrooms, washed and sliced
1 tablespoon tomato purée
6 tablespoons double cream
Salt and pepper to taste
1 pound fresh pasta (quills are good)

In an 8-quart heavy-bottomed pot, fry the onions, chilies, and garlic in the oil for a few minutes until the onion is soft. Add the canned tomatoes and simmer until most of the liquid has evaporated. Add the mushrooms and simmer for a few more minutes until they are just about soft. Stir in the tomato purée and cream. Add a little water if necessary. Heat through and season to taste.

Cook the pasta until it is al dente, stir in the sauce, and serve with a green salad and some warm ciabatta.

Jane Sales

Nutritional Information

Per serving: Calories: 256, Protein: 10 gm., Fat: 12 gm., Carbohydrates: 50 gm.

Peanut Chili Noodles

Yield: 6 servings

A cool, marinated cucumber salad would be a lovely accompaniment to these spicy noodles.

1 pound pasta: spaghetti, fettuccine, soba, or other noodles
3 tablespoons oil
6 dried red chili peppers (more or less, depending on your taste)
⅓ cup chopped peanuts
5 cloves garlic, minced
6 fresh chili peppers (red, green, and/or orange), seeded and finely chopped
2 tablespoons soy sauce
Pinch of black pepper
Scallions, sliced
Cilantro leaves, chopped

Cook the pasta according to the package directions.

While the pasta is cooking, heat the oil in a skillet on low. Add the whole dried chilies to the oil, stirring constantly. When the chilies are almost black and the oil is fragrant, remove the chilies and discard. Add the peanuts and stir a bit longer until the nuts are lightly browned. Add the garlic and fresh chili peppers, and cook for a few seconds. Remove from the heat and stir in the soy sauce and black pepper. When the pasta is cooked, drain thoroughly. Add the chili mixture to the pasta, and toss well to combine. Serve hot garnished with the scallions and cilantro leaves.

Karen Mintzias
km@salata.com

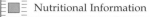 Nutritional Information

Per serving: Calories: 242,
Protein: 7 gm., Fat: 10 gm.,
Carbohydrates: 29 gm.

Linguini in Spicy Peanut Sauce

Yield: 4 to 6 servings

This is very quick to make, especially using capellini (capelli angeli or angel hair pasta), a very thin pasta that cooks in just a couple of minutes.

1 pound capellini, linguini, or similar pasta
1 cup peanut butter
1 cup hot water
¼ cup soy sauce
¼ cup white vinegar
3 to 6 scallions, finely chopped
2 to 3 cloves garlic, finely minced
1 tablespoon sugar
1 teaspoon or more hot red pepper flakes

Unless using capellini, start the pasta. Blend the peanut butter with most of the water. Stir in the soy sauce and vinegar to make a purée. Add half of the scallions, the garlic, sugar, and hot red pepper flakes. Add the rest of the hot water to achieve a sauce-like consistency. Combine with the hot pasta in a heated bowl, and garnish with the remainder of the scallions.

Bob Bland
bland@sover.net
www.sover.net/~bland

 Nutritional Information

Per serving: Calories: 461, Protein: 17 gm., Fat: 23 gm., Carbohydrates: 44 gm.

Farfalle E Fagioli

Yield: 4 to 6 servings

1 cup fresh or frozen Italian fagioli or navy beans

12 ounces farfalle or other sauce-friendly pasta, such as shells

⅓ cup sherry, or 1 to 2 tablespoons olive oil

1 red onion, chopped (about ½ cup)

2 to 3 cloves garlic, chopped

1 to 2 jalapeños, sliced (optional)

2 pints canned tomatoes, or 4 cups, chopped fresh

2 teaspoons oregano

1 teaspoon ground cumin

1 cup fresh or frozen corn kernels

½ cup black olives, sliced (optional)

Parmesan, grated (optional)

Monterey Jack cheese (optional)

Simmer the beans in enough water to cover until soft. Cook the pasta according to package directions. Heat the sherry or oil in a 2-quart saucepan. Add the onion, garlic, and jalapeños, and sauté until softened. Add the tomatoes, oregano, cumin, corn, and cooked beans, and cook for another 3 to 4 minutes. Add the olives and sprinkle with Parmesan, if desired.

If serving as is, heat another minute or two, until the olives are warmed. Spread over the pasta with a sprinkling of Parmesan, if desired. Otherwise, put the pasta in a casserole dish, toss with the sauce, and top with Jack cheese, if desired. Bake for 10 minutes or more at 350°F, until the cheese is melted.

The casserole may be assembled in advance and warmed for 2 minutes before serving.

Bob Bland
bland@sover.net
www.sover.net/~bland

Nutritional Information

Per serving: Calories: 217,
Protein: 8 gm., Fat: 0 gm.,
Carbohydrates: 41 gm.

Pasta Arrabbiata

Yield: 4 servings

I first had this dish in a little tratorria in Venice, and this is my attempt at recreating it from American sources. We were bicycling around Northern Italy and, of course, sampling both the cuisine and the wine. I found most of the northern pastas bland compared to the more interesting southern sauces I had experienced in the past, but Venice, with its historic ties to the Levant, defied that lack of spicyness.

1½ cups water
8 to 12 sun-dried tomato halves
⅓ cup sherry, or 1 to 2 teaspoons olive oil
2 to 3 cloves garlic, minced
⅓ cup minced shallots, (2 medium)
1 to 2 jalapeños, chipotles, or 1 to 2 tablespoons red pepper flakes
4 medium ripe tomatoes, or 1 pint canned
12 ounces rotini, shells, or other medium pasta
¼ cup chopped, fresh basil and/or parsley

Heat the water to a boil, and add the sun-dried tomato halves. Cook for a minute, remove from the heat, and let soak for ½ hour. Drain.

Heat the sherry or oil in a 1½-quart saucepan. Add the garlic and shallots, and sauté for 3 minutes. Add the sun-dried tomatoes, jalapeños, and tomatoes. Cook, stirring occasionally, for 20 minutes.

Start the pasta water and schedule the pasta cooking time for al dente pasta to be ready when the sauce is complete. Drain the pasta and add the sauce. Sprinkle with the fresh basil and/or parsley.

Bob Bland
bland@sover.net
www.sover.net/~bland

 Nutritional Information

Per serving: Calories: 184,
Protein: 5 gm., Fat: 0 gm.,
Carbohydrates: 34 gm.

Capellini Alla Puglia

Yield: 4 to 6 servings

Puglia is the toe of the Italian boot. It is filled with olive trees and is the major source of Italian olive oil. I don't remember where I picked up this concept. We bicycled all over the area, and I have many positive food memories, but this was more my creation of an homage to the province than a specific reference. Although Tuscan oil has a better reputation, I still buy the Puglian (extra-virgin, of course) because I feel like it comes from a tree that I have seen! Capellini is best in this dish because it absorbs the olive oil so quickly and then feeds it back to you slowly. I've never tried this with anything other than pine nuts and doubt it would work with other nuts, except perhaps chopped hazelnuts.

1 to 2 tablespoons olive oil for sautéing
2 to 3 cloves garlic, sliced
2 red bell peppers, chopped
4 to 8 scallions (optional)
¼ cup pine nuts
¼ cup capers (preferably the larger Spanish type)
½ cup halved black olives
¼ cup chopped, fresh basil (optional)
10 to 12 ounces capellini or other light pasta
Parmesan cheese to taste

Heat water for the pasta. Heat the olive oil moderately in a skillet. Add the garlic and stir a couple of times. Add the bell peppers and scallion bottoms, and stir until the garlic is golden. Add the pine nuts and stir until they just begin to turn golden. Add the capers and scallion tops, and stir a couple of times until the sizzling slows. Add the olives and basil, stir, and turn off the heat. Cook the pasta about 2 minutes or until al dente.

Drain the pasta, place in a plate or bowl, and swirl in a bit of olive oil. Cover with the sauce and grate some fresh Parmesan on top.

Bob Bland
bland@sover.net
www.sover.net/~bland

Nutritional Information

Per serving: Calories: 186,
Protein: 4 gm., Fat: 10 gm.,
Carbohydrates: 19 gm.

Saffron & Spinach Fettuccine

Yield: 3 to 4 servings

Saffron is the spice of the gods. The pollen of a particular species of crocus, it costs about the same per ounce as gold but tastes a lot better. Since it keeps fresh for years, you can splurge once in a while and buy a tiny packet.

The Saffron Butter:
Generous pinch saffron threads, soaked in hot water
3 tablespoons unsalted butter
1 shallot, minced
1 tablespoon chopped, fresh marjoram or basil
1 tablespoon chopped parsley
Pinch cayenne
Grated peel of ½ lemon or ¼ orange

The Pasta and Vegetables:
10 to 12 ounces fettuccine or other heavy pasta
1 red onion, quartered and thinly sliced (about ½ cup)
1 to 2 tablespoons olive oil
1 red bell pepper
¼ cup pine nuts or almonds
1 to 2 cloves garlic, minced
1 cup vegetable stock
2 cups spinach, stems removed and cut into wide strips
¼ teaspoon black pepper
Parmesan for garnish

Soak the saffron and bring the butter to room temperature. Cream the butter with the saffron, shallot, marjoram or basil, parsley, cayenne, and citrus peel. Cover and set aside.

Start the pasta. In a saucepan, sauté the onion in the olive oil for 1 minute. Add the bell pepper and sauté another minute. Add the nuts and garlic, and sauté until the nuts are golden. Add the stock and cook another minute. Add the spinach and stir until the spinach wilts. Lower the heat and add all but 1 tablespoon of the saffron butter. Adjust the liquid to make the mixture saucy. Drain the pasta and add to the vegetables along with the rest of the saffron butter. Season with black pepper and toss. Garnish with Parmesan.

Bob Bland
bland@sover.net
www.sover.net/~bland

Nutritional Information

Per serving: Calories: 334,
Protein: 7 gm., Fat: 20 gm.,
Carbohydrates: 28 gm.

Vegetable Pita Pizza for One

Yield: 1 serving

1 cup fresh spinach
1 teaspoon olive oil
1 clove garlic, minced
½ cup sliced zucchini
½ cup sliced mushrooms
1 sun-dried tomato, sliced
Pinch each: basil, Italian
    seasoning, salt, and pepper
2 tablespoons spicy pizza sauce
1 (6-inch) pita bread
2 tablespoons shredded low-fat
    Monterey Jack
2 tablespoons shredded low-fat
    mozzarella

Preheat the oven to 425°F. Steam the spinach until wilted. Heat the olive oil in a nonstick pan, and stir-fry the garlic, zucchini, mushrooms, sun-dried tomato, basil, Italian seasoning, salt, and pepper for 3 minutes. Stir in the spinach and cook for another minute. Spread the pizza sauce on the pita bread, and place the vegetable mixture on top. Then sprinkle the Monterey Jack and mozzarella cheeses on top of the vegetables. Place the assembled pita pizza on a nonstick cookie sheet, and bake for 5 minutes or until the cheeses are melted.

Cecilia W. Tse

Nutritional Information

Per serving: Calories: 333,
Protein: 17 gm., Fat: 11 gm.,
Carbohydrates: 42 gm.

Quick Focaccia with Red Pepper Topping

Yield: 8 servings

This takes 45 minutes from deciding to make it to sinking your teeth into the first slice. It is a little like a pizza with heavy emphasis on the crust.

1 package dry yeast (1 scant tablespoon)
½ teaspoon sugar
½ cup warm water
1 teaspoon oregano
1 teaspoon sage
2 teaspoons basil
1 tablespoon olive oil
½ cup cold water
1 teaspoon garlic powder
3 cups flour
1½ tablespoons sugar
Pinch of salt

Red Pepper Topping:
½ cup chopped red bell pepper
1½ to 2 ounces grated Parmesan
½ tablespoon olive oil
2 cloves garlic, peeled

Sprinkle the yeast and ½ teaspoon sugar over the warm water. Stir and set aside until foamy. Meanwhile, put the spices and 1 tablespoon oil in a small saucepan. Simmer over low heat for 1 minute. Remove from the heat, and stir in the cold water and yeast mixture. Place the flour, sugar, and salt in a food processor bowl. With the motor running, pour the liquid mixture through the feed tube in a steady stream as fast as the flour will absorb it. (Watch out—it's easy to spill.) Once the dough forms a ball, process 30 seconds more. Remove the dough; it will be sticky. Place in an oiled bowl, and cover loosely with a towel. Let stand 15 minutes to relax the gluten.

To make the Red Pepper Topping, chop the peppers 10 seconds in the food processor. With the motor running, add the garlic and process 10 seconds more. Add the Parmesan, pulse 3 times to mix, and process 30 seconds more. Remove the metal blade, add the oil, and mix.

Set an oven rack in the center of the oven, and preheat to 450°F.

Oil a 15½ x 10½-inch jelly-roll pan.

 Nutritional Information

Per serving: Calories: 194, Protein: 5 gm., Fat: 3 gm., Carbohydrates: 36 gm.

Pat the dough evenly with lightly floured hands to cover the bottom of the pan. Spread the topping evenly over the dough. Make slight indentations with your thumbs every 2 inches across the dough. Bake 10 to 12 minutes, or until browned.

This is also very nice made with salsa fresca (pico de gallo) instead of red peppers.

Ruth Fink-Winter
wfink@iastate.edu

Roasted Eggplant Focaccia

Yield: 16 servings

I made this one up for a pool party once; it was a big hit!

6 to 8 cloves garlic
1 cup olive oil
¼ cup red wine vinegar
2 tablespoons dried basil
2 tablespoons marjoram
1 medium-sized eggplant (1½ pounds)
1 large red bell pepper
1 large green bell pepper
2 sheets plain focaccia (purists can make it from scratch)
1 large red onion, quartered and thinly sliced
1 (6-ounce) jar artichoke hearts
Handful of sun-dried tomatoes, soaked and cut in half (okay, I admit it; this can be classified as yuppie food)
Cook's choice of red or white wine

Peel, crush, and chop 4 to 6 cloves of the garlic. In a mixing bowl, combine the garlic with the olive oil, vinegar, basil, and marjoram.

Cut the ends off the eggplant, split it lengthwise, and slice into ¼-inch thick slices. Dip each piece in the oil mixture, and arrange on a foil-covered baking pan. Broil until soft, turning once.

Core the red and green bell peppers, slice into strips, and cut the strips in half. Toss them into the oil mixture, then scoop out and place them on another foil-covered baking pan. After the eggplant is done, broil the peppers, stirring occasionally, until soft (the kitchen smells really good about now). Have some wine.

Peel the red onion and slice thinly, then break up the slices. Crush a couple of the remaining cloves of garlic, and rub them on the top of the focaccia. Scatter some sun-dried tomatoes on each bread, then loosely cover with a layer of onion. Arrange the eggplant to mostly cover, then scatter the roasted peppers. Then add some artichoke hearts, scoop the remaining garlic from the oil, and scatter that across the top. Admire the pretty colors. Have some wine.

 Nutritional Information

Per serving: Calories: 232, Protein: 4 gm., Fat: 13 gm., Carbohydrates: 23 gm.

Place the focaccia on baking pans, and bake uncovered at 350°F for about 20 minutes. Then pull them out, take another baking pan, and use it to press lightly so that all of the veggies merge together just a little. Let cool, cover with foil, and refrigerate overnight. The next day it can be heated or served cold. I cut it into slices about 3 inches square. Serve with sunshine, fresh air, and about 5 gallons of margaritas.

Chuck Narad

Cabbage Pizza

Yield: 4 servings

This is an unusual, but absolutely delicious, alternative to standard pizza varieties. I buy convenient whole wheat pizza crust in the freezer section of my health food store. Follow the manufacturer's instructions to determine whether or not to thaw the pizza crust before baking.

1 onion, minced
3 cloves garlic, minced
2 tablespoons oil
4 cups chopped cabbage
1 tablespoon fennel seed
1 cup tomato sauce
½ cup freshly grated Parmesan cheese
1 prepared whole wheat pizza crust

In a frying pan, sauté the onion and garlic in the oil for 5 minutes, or until soft. Add the cabbage and fennel seeds, stir well, and cover. Cook over medium-low heat until the cabbage is just wilted.

Preheat the oven to 425°F.

Place the pizza crust on a greased baking sheet, and top with the tomato sauce, then the cabbage mixture. Sprinkle with the Parmesan cheese. Bake for 15 to 20 minutes, or until the cheese is lightly browned.

Nanette Blanchard
76702.3406@compuserve.com

Nutritional Information

Per serving: Calories: 254,
Protein: 9 gm., Fat: 11 gm.,
Carbohydrates: 30 gm.

Vegan Moussaka

Yield: 6 to 8 servings

This is my recipe for moussaka, which I guess is fairly ethnically unsound.

2 large eggplants (aubergines),
   sliced ¼-inch thick lengthways
½ cup olive oil
3 medium potatoes, sliced
1 large onion, chopped
3 cloves garlic, minced
2 medium zucchini (courgettes),
   diced
½ cup textured vegetable
   protein, rehydrated in ½ cup
   boiling water or stock
1 large (28-ounce) can tomatoes
3 tablespoons pine nuts
3 tablespoons vegan cheese,
   grated

White Sauce:
¼ cup olive oil
¼ cup flour
2½ cups soya milk

Michael Traub traub@mistral.co.uk

Sprinkle the eggplant slices liberally with salt, and let stand for 2 hours to remove any bitterness. Rinse well and fry in a little olive oil until tender. Remove from the pan. Boil the potato slices in water for a couple of minutes, and drain well. In the same pan used for the eggplant slices, fry the potatoes in a little more olive oil until tender.

Fry the onion in a little oil until tender, then add the garlic and zucchini. Add the rehydrated textured vegetable protein, tomatoes, pine nuts, and cheese. You may like to add some herbs here, though this wasn't done traditionally.

To make the white sauce, combine ¼ cup olive oil with the flour in a medium saucepan. Heat over medium until it starts to bubble, stirring constantly. Remove from the heat and gradually whisk in soya milk, a little at a time to avoid creating lumps.

Preheat the oven to 350°F (180°C).

Make layers of the eggplant slices, tomato mixture, potatoes, and white sauce in a 9 x 13-inch baking dish. Make sure the top layer is comprised of potatoes and white sauce.

Bake in the oven for about 25 minutes.

Nutritional Information

Per serving: Calories: 440,
Protein: 10 gm., Fat: 27 gm.,
Carbohydrates: 39 gm.

Five-Chef Enchilada Thing Casserole

Yield: 6 servings

So in the middle of the party, a friend is in the kitchen planning some kind of enchilada casserole, when we each troop through to offer our opinions and then go back to the pool. The resulting casserole was pretty good, although we don't quite know what it is . . . so we call it . . . 5-chef enchilada thing casserole.

1 onion, diced
1 tablespoon olive oil
2 (10-ounce) cans green enchilada sauce
1 cup fresh tomato salsa
2 to 3 cups grated Monterey Jack and cheddar cheese
1 (15-ounce) can garbanzo beans, drained
1 (4½-ounce) can whole roasted jalapeño peppers
2 zucchini, sliced and sautéed
1 dozen whole wheat chapatis or flour tortillas
Cumin
Lots of fresh minced garlic
5 chefs

Sauté the onion in the olive oil in a small saucepan until tender. Coat the bottom of a large, lightly greased baking pan with some of the enchilada sauce. Cover with 3 chapatis. Add a layer of cheese, then a layer of zucchini, then a layer of salsa (with the cumin and garlic added), and 3 more chapatis. Then some green sauce, some more cheese, a layer of onions, the garbanzos, and 3 more chapatis. More salsa, the rest of the zucchini, more cheese, the jalapeños, and the rest of the chapatis. Cover with the rest of the green sauce, and bake at 400°F for about 45 minutes, maybe an hour, until it starts to form a golden brown crust. Let cool for about 10 minutes, then slice and serve.

Be sure to follow this recipe exactly or it won't come out! :-) Yeah, right.

Chuck Narad

Nutritional Information

Per serving: Calories: 448, Protein: 18 gm., Fat: 14 gm., Carbohydrates: 58 gm.

Brazilian Bean Casserole

Yield: 6 servings

Black beans rule native cuisines from Cuba to Brazil. They have a much stronger taste than pintos or kidney beans; using the milder Jack cheese allows the strong black bean flavor to come through.

2 to 3 cups cooked black beans
1 onion, chopped (about ½ cup)
2 to 3 cloves garlic, minced
1 tablespoon olive oil, or ⅓ cup sherry
2 pints canned tomatoes, or more than 2 pints chopped fresh tomatoes
1 to 2 jalapeños, chopped
1 tablespoon oregano
1 teaspoon ground cumin
1 teaspoon ground coriander
1 teaspoon black pepper
2 cups Monterey Jack, grated
¼ cup chopped, fresh cilantro, or 1 tablespoon dried

Make sure the beans are tender. Sauté the onion and garlic in the olive oil for 5 minutes. Add the tomatoes, jalapeños, oregano, cumin, coriander, and a grinding of fresh black pepper. Cook, stirring frequently, about 5 minutes. Add the beans to the skillet, and stir. Preheat the oven to 375°F. Put the mixture in a casserole dish, and cover with the cheese. Bake for 20 to 25 minutes or until the cheese is golden. Garnish with the cilantro.

Bob Bland
bland@sover.net
www.sover.net/~bland

Nutritional Information

Per serving: Calories: 295,
Protein: 17 gm., Fat: 13 gm.,
Carbohydrates: 25 gm.

Stuffed Cabbage

Yield: 8 to 10 servings

I started with my mom's recipe, but instead of meat I used walnuts, mushrooms, and tomatoes. It wasn't until I got the whole dish together that I realized it has a wonderful interplay of sweet and sour. Make plenty; you'll eat more than you realize, and you can always freeze the leftovers. This may be the path to nirvana. (Is the path to nirvana through a person's stomach?)

2 heads of cabbage
1½ cups uncooked brown rice
  (I used brown basmati)
¾ cup raisins
½ pound oyster mushrooms,
  sliced into small chunks
¾ cup coarsely chopped walnuts
1 cup brown sugar (you might
  want to try maple sugar or
  syrup if refined sugar bothers
  you)
1 cup lemon juice
2 large onions, chopped
2 (15-ounce) cans stewed
  tomatoes
1 cup water
Salt and pepper to taste

Bring a large pot of water to a boil. Core the cabbage. Take the pot off of the heat, drop in a cabbage, and let set for 10 to 15 minutes. Drop the cabbage into a colander to cool a few minutes, then carefully pull off whole leaves, and set them aside. You should get 12 to 16 leaves per head. Repeat with the second head. Set aside the remainder of the cabbage.

Combine the rice, raisins, mushrooms, walnuts, brown sugar, ½ cup of the lemon juice, ⅔ of the onion, and 1 can of tomatoes (drain off the juice and reserve it).

Place approximately 2 to 3 tablespoons of the rice mixture onto the thick end of a cabbage leaf, fold in the sides, and roll towards the tip. Place seam-side down in a 6-quart Dutch oven. Repeat until all of the cabbage leaves are stuffed (they will stack up to nearly fill the pot).

Chop up the remaining cabbage into a bowl (my mother called this the "shmatas," which means "rags"). Add the second can of tomatoes, the reserved juice from the first can, the remaining lemon

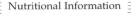
Nutritional Information

Per serving: Calories: 301,
Protein: 5 gm., Fat: 6 gm.,
Carbohydrates: 56 gm.

juice, onion, salt, and pepper, and any remaining filling. Mix and pour on top of the rolls in the pot. Add about 1 cup of water (won't quite cover it).

Heat on medium until the mixture boils, then cover and reduce the heat to medium-low. Cook 3 to 4 hours, reducing the heat to low if necessary. The rolls are done when the grains of rice in the extra filling are soft. The rolls steam in the juices, and shrink down as the cabbage cooks. Don't stir!

You can then serve immediately, or reheat the next day. These reheat and freeze well. To serve, spoon 2 to 3 rolls onto a plate, add some shmatas and juices, and serve with Russian rye bread (to mop up the juice). Eat and repeat until unconscious.

Chuck Narad

Tofu Piccata

Yield: 6 to 8 servings

This is an original recipe adapted from when I was a flesh eater. I am now vegan and that is how all food prepared in my home is served. The tofu substitution was at the suggestion of my "meat eating" fiancé, so if any credits/dedications are in order, this would be to my: "meat eating someone special" or as a friend says "MESS."

2 pounds firm tofu
½ cup flour
2 teaspoons salt
1 teaspoon pepper
1½ tablespoons garlic granules
⅓ to ½ cup olive oil
1 (14-ounce) can vegetable broth
  or 2 cups homemade broth
¾ cup lemon juice
2 tablespoons dried parsley

Begin by rinsing the tofu in the tub it comes in. Drain as best you can. Then cut each block into 4 pieces (cut through the short dimension, not the long). I use 2 cookie sheets for pressing. Take a good amount of paper towels or clean kitchen towels, and lay them on one cookie sheet. Then place all the rinsed and sliced tofu on the towels. Take another good amount of towels, and place them on top of the tofu. Place the other cookie sheet on top of the tofu and towels. Place something heavy on the top cookie sheet. I have used the leaf from the dining room table, a case of beer, just about anything that is fairly heavy. Let the tofu press for 30 to 45 minutes. At that point, you will have to do a towel change, and press the tofu again. If you have the time, you could even do this a third time, but two times usually works fine. This can be done a day or two ahead, and the tofu will be even firmer after being refrigerated.

On a flat plate, combine the flour, salt, pepper, and garlic powder, and mix well. Reserve 2 tablespoons of this mixture, and set aside. Then take the tofu, piece by

 Nutritional Information

Per serving: Calories: 244,
Protein: 10 gm., Fat: 16 gm.,
Carbohydrates: 10 gm.

piece, and coat well with the flour mixture. I pat it on quite well.

Take one large frying pan (a 12-inch pan if you have one), and put in about ¼ cup olive oil. When the oil is hot, put in the tofu pieces, and brown them on each side. I turn them a couple or three times.

Take the tofu out of the pan, and put it on a plate. To the pan, add the vegetable broth, lemon juice, the reserved flour mixture, and parsley.

Bring to a fast simmer, and add the tofu. Turn down the heat so the tofu in the broth/juice mixture simmers slowly.

I turn the tofu a few times while it is simmering. This part of the dish takes about 15 minutes or until you are sure everything is hot all the way through.

While the tofu is in the simmering phase, boil up some spiral pasta, and steam some broccoli, if you would like.

The final dish is served as such: pasta on the plate, tofu on the pasta, pan broth/juice mixture on the tofu, and broccoli on the plate. The broth/juice mixture is wonderful on the pasta and broccoli.

The items that can be massaged to taste would be the salt, pepper, garlic powder, and lemon juice.

You could cut the amount of olive oil as well, but you do need a good enough amount to brown the tofu pieces, and it is a good flavoring agent with the broth.

A nice green salad and some sourdough or crusty French bread are good with this meal too. And the leftovers age splendidly.

Krissie Griffiths
krissie@chicago.com

Egg-Roll Shepherd's Pie

Yield: 4 servings

Ever have one of those meals that sort of evolves while you are cooking it? I started out daydreaming about mashed potatoes with various veggies in it while driving home last night, but it took on a few twists in the kitchen. The result was a simple and hearty main dish which took about an hour to prepare. It is lacto but can be made vegan with a few omissions (margarine for butter, skip the yogurt).

As always, proportions are approximate and contents listed are what I found staining the counter this morning; YMMV (Your Meal May Vary).

7 new potatoes (pink skinned), whole with skin
1 tablespoon oil
3 cloves garlic, minced
1 small onion, chopped
½ pound sliced mushrooms
¼ head cabbage, shredded
Splash of white wine
1 large carrot, grated
Small handful of sunflower seeds (about ¼ cup or more)
½ cup raisins
1 tablespoon hoisin sauce*
2 tablespoons butter or margarine
½ cup nonfat yogurt
Pepper to taste

Hoisin sauce is a sweet, reddish-brown sauce made from soybeans—often used as a dipping sauce. Look for it in Asian groceries.

Cook the potatoes in their skins (either boil them, or puncture and microwave).

Meanwhile, heat the oil in a skillet over medium heat. Sauté the garlic, then the onion until soft. Add the mushrooms and sauté until they shrink a bit. Add the cabbage, then a splash or three of white wine, and continue stirring until the cabbage softens a bit. Add the carrot, sunflower seeds, raisins, and hoisin sauce, stir, and set aside.

Preheat the oven to 350°F.

(At this point I thought, wow! This is a great filling for egg rolls, it just needs some black fungus and a touch of soy sauce. Nah, I have those potatoes ready. Hmmm . . . add some lotus leaf and hoisin sauce, perfect filling for mu-shu. Nah, I have those potatoes ready. Hey, mash with the potatoes, a bit of cumin, coriander, and turmeric, and wrap it in those whole wheat chapatis! Nah, I already preheated the oven. Guess I'll make a shepherd's pie.)

Mash the potatoes with a hand masher (not too smooth, the chunks of skin should still be

Nutritional Information

Per serving: Calories: 479, Protein: 8 gm., Fat: 14 gm., Carbohydrates: 79 gm.

noticeable); add the butter and yogurt, and season with pepper.

Spread the mushroom/cabbage mixture with all the juices in a 9 x 9-inch pyrex baking dish. Cover with the potato mixture, and smooth it out. Bake for 30 minutes, let cool for about 5 minutes, and serve. Heavy bread and a green salad would be good accompaniments.

Enjoy!

Chuck Narad

Spanish Scrambled Tofu

Yield: 4 servings

3 large potatoes, cut in ½-inch cubes
5 tablespoons olive oil
3 cloves garlic, minced
1 medium onion, chopped
1 green bell pepper, chopped
1 red bell pepper, chopped
½ cup corn
1 (10½-ounce) package crumbled, extra-firm silken tofu (340 gm)
1⅓ cups soya yogurt (300 ml)
1 teaspoon egg replacer
Salt and pepper to taste
1 teaspoon turmeric
1 teaspoon vegetable stock powder, or 1 cube vegetable bouillon
¼ cup soya milk

Sauté the potatoes in the olive oil in a covered frying pan over low heat until soft, loosening occasionally with a metal spatula. Add the garlic and onion, cover, and simmer until soft. Add the bell peppers, and continue to cook until soft.

While the vegetables are cooking, combine the remaining ingredients in a medium mixing bowl. Add to the sautéed vegetables, cover, and cook until the tofu is starting to brown. If necessary, cook uncovered to remove excess moisture.

The potatoes and bell peppers can be replaced with mushrooms and/or cabbage, if you prefer.

Michael Traub
traub@mistral.co.uk

Nutritional Information

Per serving: Calories: 403, Protein: 14 gm., Fat: 20 gm., Carbohydrates: 39 gm.

Vegetarian Paella

Yield: 6 servings

This rich, all-vegetable version of the colorful Spanish dish uses saffron. It is an expensive spice but only a small amount is needed. For the best flavor, look for saffron threads and crush them between your fingers instead of using powdered saffron.

1 onion, chopped
1 serrano chile pepper, finely
    chopped
1 red bell pepper, chopped
1 green bell pepper, chopped
1 tablespoon olive oil
3 cloves garlic, minced
½ teaspoon saffron threads,
    crumbled into powder
½ teaspoon paprika
1 cup uncooked converted rice
3 cups water
1½ teaspoons lemon zest
1 (15-ounce) can garbanzo
    beans, rinsed and drained
1 cup frozen peas
14 ounces artichoke hearts in
    water, drained

Preheat the oven to 375°F.

In a large paella pan or oven-proof stock pot, sauté the onion, serrano chile, and red and green bell peppers in the olive oil over medium-high heat for 7 minutes. Add the garlic, saffron, and paprika, and cook an additional 3 minutes. Add the rice, water, lemon zest, garbanzo beans, peas, and artichoke hearts, and cover. Bake for 25 minutes, or until the rice is tender.

Nanette Blanchard
76702.3406@compuserve.com

 Nutritional Information

Per serving: Calories: 265,
Protein: 9 gm., Fat: 3 gm.,
Carbohydrates: 47 gm.

Asparagus/Mushroom Casserole

Yield: 6 servings

Costco had big wads of asparagus on sale this week, so I decided to play around with new ideas. This one came out pretty good.

2½ cups cooked brown rice
1 pound asparagus, cut into 2-inch pieces
½ pound mushrooms, chopped
1 medium onion, chopped (1½ cups)
¼ cup cashews or sunflower seeds
4 eggs
4 cloves garlic, minced
1 teaspoon black pepper
1 teaspoon marjoram
½ cup grated Swiss or mozzarella cheese
butter or margarine (to grease the pan)

Preheat the oven to 375°F. Then mix everything except the cheese in a large mixing bowl until well combined. Pour into a greased 8 x 12-inch baking pan, and sprinkle the cheese on top. Bake for 40 minutes.

Chuck Narad

 Nutritional Information

Per serving: Calories: 252, Protein: 11 gm., Fat: 8 gm., Carbohydrates: 31 gm.

Red Lentil Curry

Yield: 6 to 8 servings

2 teaspoons cumin
½ teaspoon turmeric
1 teaspoon paprika
1 large onion, chopped
2 cloves garlic, minced
1 tablespoon vegetable oil
1 fresh red chilli
¼ teaspoon black pepper
1 cup dried red lentils
1 cup water
1 (28-ounce) can tomatoes
1 tablespoon tamarind sauce
2 tablespoons chopped fresh
  cilantro
¼ cup apple juice
Salt to taste
Juice of 1 lemon

Fry the cumin, turmeric, paprika, onion, and garlic in the oil. Add the chilli, black pepper, and red lentils. Fry for a couple more minutes.

Add the water, canned tomatoes, tamarind sauce, and cilantro, and simmer for about 30 to 45 minutes. The lentils should be soft but still intact. Add the apple juice and salt. Simmer for 10 more minutes until the lentils are disintegrating and the mixture has thickened. Stir in the fresh lemon juice, and serve with brown rice topped with soya yogurt.

Michael Traub
traub@mistral.co.uk

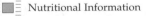

Nutritional Information

Per serving: Calories: 117,
Protein: 6 gm., Fat: 1 gm.,
Carbohydrates: 19 gm.

75

Four-Mushroom Thai Curry

Yield: 4 to 6 servings

Thai curries are especially fragrant; in addition to the usual curry spices, they contain lemon grass and coconut milk. Thai curry tends to be hot (hey, I like food that makes me sweat!), but the coconut milk tempers the heat, allowing other flavors through. If you like hotter curries (3 or 4 star, as they say in Thai restaurants), add a small amount of Vietnamese "tuong ot" (garlic-chili paste) to the sauce before adding it to the wok. The basic recipe here is infinitely variable; this is a version I made for a crowd one night.

Sorry about all of the cans, but most of this stuff is not available fresh; if you have access to a good Asian grocery, many of the cans disappear.

1½ cups seitan, drained and cut into ½-inch cubes
1 can water chestnuts, sliced
1 (8-ounce) can bamboo shoots (or a chunk of fresh), sliced
1 (15-ounce) can straw mushrooms, drained, rinsed, and sliced
1 (15-ounce) can golden button mushrooms, drained and rinsed
1 small handful dried black fungus
1 cup fresh oyster mushrooms, or 1 (15-ounce) can, sliced
1 to 2 tablespoons yellow Thai curry paste
1 bunch fresh basil
1 (14-ounce) can coconut milk
1 stalk lemon grass, cut into 1-inch sections (optional)
Peanut or olive oil
Thai sweet chili sauce (optional)
1 clove of garlic, minced (optional)

Nutritional Information

Per serving: Calories: 335,
Protein: 18 gm., Fat: 16 gm.,
Carbohydrates: 25 gm.

Soak the black fungus in a bowl of warm water for about 20 minutes while prepping the vegetables. Marinate the seitan in Thai sweet chili sauce, if you want to (available in Asian markets as a chicken marinade), just enough to get all of the chunks wet; stir occasionally. Open, drain, and slice all of the canned ingredients; slice the fresh ones to stir-fry size.

Remove most of the stems from the basil, and chop the remainder of the basil coarsely. Heat ¼ cup of oil in a small pot, add the curry paste, and stir-fry it for a few minutes. Add the basil, stir until it wilts, then stir in the coconut milk, and reduce the heat to low. Stir this occasionally while stir-frying the vegetables.

Drain and rinse the black fungus, and cut into strips if necessary.

Heat the wok, then add 1 to 2 tablespoons oil; add the garlic (if desired), then stir-fry the seitan for a few minutes. Next, add each

cooking sake
and your choice among: carrots, broccoli, onion, zucchini, cut into stir-fry size pieces.

of the other ingredients, from firmest to lightest, stirring each for a minute or two before adding the next.

Every 2 to 3 ingredients, add a splash of sake to the wok for sweet steam. When the vegetables are almost ready, pour the curry sauce over them, and stir for a few minutes. Serve over basmati or calrose rice.

Prep time: about 40 minutes, unless the rice takes longer.

Chuck Narad

Two-Day Satay Tofu Kabobs with Peanut Sauce

Yield: 8 servings

Well, after Guru cooked us up a Southern Indian feast a couple of weeks ago, I got draft-ed to do something Thai for the crowd. Since a large crowd (4 became 7 became 10) was coming, it only seemed fair that at least one dish was a total experiment. I decided to do a Thai veggie curry, fried rice, something new and exciting—Satay Tofu Kabobs, fruit salad with yogurt/amaretto sauce to round it out, and lots of wine . . .

The tofu dish took two days to prepare, which got me thinking about the time I was on the island of Espiritu Santo in Vanuatu. The country is still very primitive; people with shells through the nose, used to be cannibals (but not in at least 20 years . . . uh HUH!). Anyway, we hired a guy with a truck to drive us to some interesting places on the island. After visiting a kastom (traditional) village that would let outsiders see them, we drove through the government agriculture station. The only industry in the island is the production of copra (coconut meat), so the station had many strains of coconut palms. It also had many varieties of kava, which is a plant that produces a mild narcot-ic which is consumed sort of like beer in many parts of the South Pacific. After cruising past dozens of rows of kava, there was a small sign: "Two-Day Kava." Yee hah! So in honor of two-day kava, I'm going to call this dish "Two-Day Satay Tofu Kabobs."

2 pounds firm tofu
½ cup light soy sauce
¼ cup extra-virgin olive oil
2 tablespoons vinegar
2 tablespoons sugar
3 cloves garlic, mashed and minced
1 teaspoon cumin
¼ teaspoon white pepper
2 tablespoons lemon juice
1 tablespoon dried onion
1 cucumber (for garnish)

(Note: In a subsequent experiment, I added 1 cup of orange juice to the mari-nade, which worked really well.)

Rinse and dry the tofu, then slice it into quarters. Put lots of paper towels on a cutting board, place the tofu (cut side down) on the towels, put several more lay-ers of towels on top, then cover with another board, and place a heavy weight on it. (I used a 2½ gallon water jug and two gallons of tequila.) This needs to sit for at least 4 hours, maybe 5. Lots of water will come out. After this, cut each piece into 3 strips (these will be something like 1 x 3 x ⅓ inches).

Mix together the soy sauce, oil, vinegar, sugar, garlic, cumin, white pepper, lemon juice, and dried onion. Place the tofu strips into a glass dish, pour the mari-nade over them, and cover. Marinate 24 to 48 hours (mostly in

Nutritional Information

Per serving: Calories: 295, Protein: 12 gm., Fat: 20 gm., Carbohydrates: 12 gm.

Sauce:

1 medium onion, minced
1 tablespoon chili oil
2 cloves garlic, minced
2 serrano chilies, seeded and
    minced
Lots of minced fresh gingerroot
    (about 4 tablespoons)
½ teaspoon cumin
1 cup water
⅓ cup peanut butter
½ (14-ounce) can coconut milk

the refrigerator).

Soak 8 bamboo skewers in cold water for 15 minutes (keeps them from incinerating when you broil them).

Take the tofu out of the marinade, and skewer them lengthwise on the skewer, 3 pieces per skewer. Go slowly and carefully so they don't split! Cover a baking pan with foil, then lay the skewers across the pan. Broil until brown and starting to bubble, then turn over and do the same on the other side.

Surround a platter with thin slices of cucumber, and arrange the skewers on top.

To make the peanut sauce, sauté the onion in the chili oil. When soft, add the garlic and chilies, and sauté another minute or so. Add the ginger, cumin, and water; when hot, add the peanut butter and coconut milk. Serve the peanut sauce on the side. (The remaining marinade can be poured on a stir-fry. Why waste all of that natural goodness?)

Chuck Narad

Thai-Fry

Yield: 4 servings

1 cup water
1 large Spanish onion, roughly chopped
2 large cloves garlic, minced
2 teaspoons freshly grated root ginger (gingerroot)
2 tablespoons crunchy peanut butter
1 teaspoon vegetable stock powder or yeast extract (Marmite)
3 tablespoons shoyu or tamari
1 pound broccoli, stalks peeled and diced, and florets separated
4 ounces tempeh, cut into small squares
¾ pound mushrooms, sliced
1 yellow bell pepper (capsicum), sliced
½ teaspoon black pepper
½ cup corn

In a large oiled wok, add the water and bring to a boil. Add the onion, and garlic, and cook until the onion is soft. Add the ginger, peanut butter, stock, and shoyu, and continue stirring until the mixture thickens. Add more water if it gets too thick or starts to burn. Add the peeled broccoli stalks and the tempeh. Then add the mushrooms, bell pepper, broccoli florets, and black pepper. Cook on high heat while stirring constantly. Add the corn and serve on a massive bed of brown rice.

Michael Traub
traub@mistral.co.uk

 Nutritional Information

Per serving: Calories: 202, Protein: 12 gm., Fat: 6 gm., Carbohydrates: 25 gm.

Lime Tempeh Stir-Fry

Yield: 4 servings

This is vaguely Indonesian and quite tasty! As usual all quantities are approximate since I rarely measure in the kitchen.

2 (8-ounce) packages tempeh

Marinade:
1 cup lime juice
⅔ cup light soy sauce
2 cups white wine
8 cloves garlic, coarsely chopped
2 tablespoons cumin

Peanut oil
1 carrot, sliced ¼ inch thick
1 small head of broccoli, cut into
    florets (about 1 cup)
1 medium onion, quartered and
    cut ½ inch thick
½ pound oyster mushrooms,
    sliced into strips

4 tablespoons Thai Peanut-Chili
    Sauce (see page 79)
2 tablespoons cornstarch
    dissolved in 1 cup warm
    water

Cut the tempeh in half the short way, then diagonally, yielding 8 triangles.

Mix the lime juice, soy sauce, white wine, garlic, and cumin into a marinade, and marinate the tempeh for a couple of hours in a roasting dish. Drain off and reserve most of the marinade, keeping a little bit in the bottom of the roasting dish. Broil the tempeh in this for about 5 minutes on each side.

Heat a wok, add a splash of peanut oil, and let heat. Quickly stir-fry the carrot, then the broccoli, and then the onion, about 1 minute each. Add the mushrooms and the reserved marinade, and stir 1 minute. Add the peanut sauce and stir 1 more minute. Then add the cornstarch and cook until it thickens.

To serve, place a mound of jasmine rice on each plate, pile the stir-fry on one side of it, arrange 2 tempeh wedges around the other side, and garnish the tempeh with the garlic chunks from the roasting dish. Pour any remaining sauce from the dish over the tempeh.

Chuck Narad

Nutritional Information

Per serving: Calories: 267,
Protein: 14 gm., Fat: 5 gm.,
Carbohydrates: 32 gm.

Utterly Udon

Yield: 2 to 3 servings

I did not become interested in udon noodles until a few years ago when a Japanese noodle shop opened near my office. I quickly learned to love them and soon found them in the local coop in both the whole wheat and brown rice versions. I have gone onto many different variations of this dish, usually depending on whatever is in the refrigerator or coming out of the garden. The Szechuan sauce I mention is a firey, soy-based sauce with lots of peppers. The final taste of this depends heavily on what soy sauce you use. I keep four or five on hand for different moods but usually come back to the sweetish Indonesian ketsap, the linguistic, if not culinary, ancestor of the modern ketchup.

1 onion, chopped (⅓ to ½ cup)
1 to 2 cloves garlic, minced
1 to 2 tablespoons peanut oil
10 to 12 ounces whole wheat or
    brown rice udon
1 teaspoon sesame oil
2 to 3 tablespoons soy or
    Szechuan sauce
Plus any of the following, the
    amounts varying with your
    choices:
Ginger, minced
Tofu, cubed
Tempeh, cut into 1-inch blocks
Carrots, chopped or sliced
Celery, sliced
Cabbage, chopped
Kim chee, chopped
Sesame seeds
Bell peppers, chopped
Bok choi, chopped
Mushrooms, chopped*
Bean sprouts*
Zucchini, sliced*
Water chestnuts, sliced*
Bamboo shoots*
Cashews*
Scallions, chopped*

quick-cooking

Start simmering water for the noodles.

In a saucepan, sauté the onions, garlic, and any long-cooking vegetables in the peanut oil until the onions are translucent (3 to 5 minutes). Add the noodles to the water. Add the medium-cooking items to the saucepan, and sauté until tender (5 minutes). Add the quick-cooking items and sesame oil, and stir a couple of times. Add the soy sauce or Szechuan sauce (which is quite hot and spicy). Serve over the cooked noodles.

Bob Bland
bland@sover.net
www.sover.net/~bland

Nutritional Information
Per serving: Calories: 147,
Protein: 12 gm., Fat: 11 gm.,
Carbohydrates: 39 gm.

82

Tempeh Cacciatore

Yield: 4 to 6 servings

1 large onion, chopped
3 cloves garlic, crushed
2 tablespoons oil
8 ounces tempeh, cubed
1 tablespoon soy sauce
1 green bell pepper, chopped
1 cup sliced mushrooms
1 teaspoon oregano
1 teaspoon basil
1 (15-ounce) can tomato sauce
1 (15-ounce) can whole
   tomatoes, drained

In a large saucepan, cook the onion and garlic in the oil for 3 to 5 minutes or until soft. Add the tempeh and soy sauce, and cook, stirring occasionally, until the tempeh is browned. Add the green bell pepper and mushrooms, and cook an additional 5 minutes over medium heat. Add the remaining ingredients, stir well, cover, and cook over low heat for 30 minutes. Serve over hot cooked pasta.

Nanette Blanchard
76702.3406@compuserve.com

 Nutritional Information

Per serving: Calories: 203,
Protein: 10 gm., Fat: 8 gm.,
Carbohydrates: 21 gm.

Tempeh Sloppy Joe

Yield: 3 to 6 servings (depending on grain choice)

1 onion, chopped (about ½ cup)
8 ounces tempeh, cut into ¼ to
 ½-inch blocks
1 to 2 teaspoons olive oil
1 pint canned tomatoes
1 green pepper, chopped
Sprinkle of red pepper flakes to
 taste
1 teaspoon ground cumin
Soy sauce to taste
Your choice of rice, grain, or
 bread

Sauté the onion and then the tempeh in the olive oil until slightly brown. Add the tomatoes, green pepper, red pepper flakes, cumin, and soy sauce. Cook for about 15 to 20 minutes over low heat. Serve over bread, rice, or other grain.

Bob Bland
bland@sover.net
www.sover.net/~bland

 Nutritional Information

Per serving: Calories: 147,
Protein: 10 gm., Fat: 5 gm.,
Carbohydrates: 16 gm.

Braised Spicy Tofu

Yield: 4 servings

I was originally going to do the tofu in a spicy black bean sauce, but I noticed that the bottle said 1990 and had been in the refrigerator since then. This sauce was thrown together on the fly. On the fry? Whatever.

1 pound firm tofu
1 tablespoon cornstarch
1 teaspoon brown miso paste
⅔ cup warm water
½ teaspoon Chinese 5-spice
  powder
2 tablespoons light soy sauce
1 tablespoon peanut oil
2 carrots, split and cut at a sharp
  angle ¼ inch thick
1 to 2 tablespoons hot oil, to
  taste
sesame oil (a few shakes from
  the bottle)
1 small zucchini, split and cut at
  a sharp angle ¼ inch thick
1 tablespoon dry sherry

Chuck Narad

Before you start cooking the rice, slice the block of tofu in half lengthwise. Place about 4 paper towels on a dinner plate. Place the two halves of the tofu on that. Top with two more paper towels, then another dinner plate (as if you were stacking the plates) or a cutting board. Place a heavy weight on top. (My standard kitchen weight is a gallon of brandy.) Let the tofu set 30 to 40 minutes. (Keep your hands off the brandy during this time!)

When you are ready to start cooking, cut the tofu into 1 x ½-inch cubes. Dissolve the cornstarch in a few tablespoons of warm water. Add the miso paste and dissolve it; then add the water, the 5-spice powder, and the soy sauce, and set aside.

Heat the peanut oil in the wok, and stir-fry the tofu for about 3 minutes. Add the carrots and stir-fry 2 minutes, adding the hot oil at the same time. Add a few shakes of sesame oil, then add the zucchini, and stir for 2 more minutes, adding the sherry. Stir the miso sauce in case it has settled, pour it over the ingredients in the wok, and stir until it thickens (this happens pretty fast).

Nutritional Information

Per serving: Calories: 200, Protein: 9 gm., Fat: 13 gm., Carbohydrates: 9 gm.

Rice With Different Stuff In It

Yield: 6 servings

This is yet another variation of my Rice With Stuff in It recipe; it is a tasty and nutritious, 30-minute one-pot casserole.

1½ cups uncooked rice (I use white basmati rice)

3 cups water

1 small onion, diced

2 cups chopped broccoli (florets and stems)

2 slices of dried pineapple, minced

4 ounces baked savory tofu* (from the store), cubed

1 cup sliced mushrooms (any variety)

Small handful of sunflower seeds

2 tablespoons garam masala (see page 33)

1 teaspoon ground cumin seed

2 teaspoons ground cardamom

1 teaspoon turmeric

½ teaspoon nutmeg

¼ teaspoon cayenne pepper

1 tablespoon miso paste

1 tablespoon margarine or butter

*I buy this at a local health food store. It is basically tofu that has been pressed, marinated in soy and spices, then baked. It's also good cold, on a sandwich with mustard, tomato, and sprouts.

Combine all the ingredients in a pot. Bring to a boil, stir, cover, and reduce the heat to medium-low. Cook for 20 minutes, no peeking! (For brown rice, cook 40 minutes.) It may form a crust on the bottom.

Serve with yogurt on the side.

Optional additions include cashews, walnuts, brown and golden raisins, dried cranberries, carrots, cauliflower, precooked and cubed potatoes, mung sprouts, or just about anything you might find in the refrigerator.

Chuck Narad

 Nutritional Information

Per serving: Calories: 222, Protein: 6 gm., Fat: 7 gm., Carbohydrates: 34 gm.

Red Beans & Rice

Yield: 4 to 6 servings

This is a classic dish from New Orleans, but their chefs usually add unnecessary flesh. For this recipe, I have consulted several sources, including a friend of a purveyor of Cajun spices in San Francisco.

2 to 3 cups cooked red, pinto, black, or kidney beans
1 to 2 small red onions, chopped (about ½ cup)
3 cloves garlic, minced
3 cups water or stock
2 bay leaves
2 teaspoons paprika
1 teaspoon each: cayenne, ground cumin, thyme, oregano, and dry mustard
½ teaspoon black pepper
½ teaspoon white pepper
1 to 2 tablespoons olive oil, or ⅓ cup sherry
1 stalk celery, sliced in ¼-inch pieces
1 green pepper, chopped into ¾-inch squares
1 cup brown rice, preferably long-grain
½ cup water

Simmer the beans in a 2-quart saucepan with half of the onions, half of the garlic, 3 cups water, and 1 bay leaf. While the beans are cooking, combine the paprika, cayenne, cumin, thyme, oregano, dry mustard, and black and white pepper in a small bowl or dish.

In a saucepan or skillet, sauté the remaining onions in the olive oil for about 1 minute. Add the garlic and cook until the onions soften, about 1 to 2 minutes more. Add the celery and green pepper, and sauté for 1 to 2 more minutes. Add the spices and cook for for about 30 more seconds.

Add the brown rice, beans, and bean liquid, plus ½ cup water or more. Bring to a boil, reduce the heat, cover, and simmer for 45 to 60 minutes until the rice is tender.

Bob Bland
bland@sover.net
www.sover.net/~bland

 Nutritional Information

Per serving: Calories: 257, Protein: 8 gm., Fat: 5 gm., Carbohydrates: 45 gm.

Spinach & Mushroom Crêpes

Yield: 4 servings (12 crêpes)

Crêpes:
2 medium or large eggs, or 3
    large egg whites
1 cup flour
¼ teaspoon salt
2 tablespoons vegetable oil
1¼ cups milk

White sauce:
3 tablespoons butter
3 tablespoons flour
¾ teaspoon salt
⅛ teaspoon cayenne (optional)
1½ cups milk

Filling:
2 to 3 tablespoons olive oil
1 onion, finely chopped (½ cup)
1 garlic clove, chopped (or more
    to taste)
½ pound mushrooms, sliced (a
    mixture of shiitake and
    button, or as desired)
1 pound fresh spinach, washed
    and cut into shreds
1 cup grated cheese (Parmesan
    or Parmesan/Swiss mixture)

To make the crêpes, mix the eggs, flour, salt, oil, and milk in a blender or food processor. Allow to set for 30 minutes to 1 hour. (This allows the flour to absorb some of the liquid.) For the smoothest crêpes, re-blend for a few seconds.

Melt a little butter in a 6 or 8-inch, nonstick or well-seasoned cast iron pan. When the pan is hot, add about 2 tablespoons of batter. Tilt the pan back and forth until the bottom is coated. Cook over medium heat until the crêpe is set. Turn and brown briefly on the other side. Stack the crêpes with wax paper between the layers. Add butter to the pan as necessary to keep the crêpes from sticking. (If you get the hang of this, you can have two pans going simultaneously. This makes the process much faster.)

To make the sauce, melt the 2 tablespoons butter in a medium saucepan, add the 2 tablespoons flour, and beat with a whisk. Add the salt, cayenne, and milk, and beat thoroughly. Heat to a simmer, stirring frequently. Simmer until thick and smooth, about 2 to 5 minutes.

To make the filling, heat the olive oil in a large skillet with a lid. Add the onion, garlic, and mush-

Nutritional Information

Per crêpe: Calories: 206,
Protein: 8 gm., Fat: 13 gm.,
Carbohydrates: 14 gm.

rooms, and sauté about 5 minutes until the onion is cooked and the mushrooms are soft. Add the spinach to the pan, cover, and cook about 3 minutes until the spinach is limp. Add about half the white sauce to the pan, and about half the cheese. Add salt and pepper to taste.

To cook, preheat the oven to 400°F. Oil a large, flat baking dish (about 9 x 13 inches). Put about 2 tablespoons filling on each crêpe, and roll up. Place the filled crêpes in the baking dish in a single layer close together. If the remaining white sauce is very thick, add about 1 tablespoon milk, and whisk to blend. Pour the white sauce over the crêpes, and sprinkle with the remaining Parmesan cheese. Bake 8 to 10 minutes until the sauce bubbles and the crêpes start to brown.

Eddie Reiter reiter@mcs.csuhayward.edu

Black Bean & Jack Cheese Burritos

Yield: 4 to 6 servings

This recipe can also be used for kidney or pinto beans and cheddar cheese can easily substitute for Jack cheese. Beans should be thoroughly cooked until they are very tender. By the way, oregano is very easy to grow and to dry. If you have a little space, you can tuck in a perennial plant, and it will produce for years. In the fall, just cut the stems, twine them together, and hang somewhere convenient, and for months you will have a taste treat every time you use the dried foliage. Far superior to the expensive stuff in the silly little bottles!

3 to 4 cups cooked black beans
1 onion, chopped (about ½ cup)
2 to 3 cloves garlic, minced
1 to 2 jalapeños, minced
1 tablespoon chopped fresh oregano, or ½ tablespoon dried
1 teaspoon ground cumin
½ teaspoon cayenne, powdered chili, or paprika
1 pint tomatoes, canned, or ½ pint fresh, chopped
8 to 12 tortillas
1 cup or more Monterey Jack cheese

The beans should be very soft. Blend the onion, garlic, and jalapeño, and divide in half. Add half the blended mixture, ½ tablespoon oregano, and the cumin to the cooked beans and reheat. Cook until the beans are thick. Sauté the remaining onions, garlic, and jalapeños in a saucepan. Add the cayenne and stir, then add the tomatoes. Cook over medium heat for about 10 minutes until reduced to a sauce-like consistency.

Preheat the oven to 350°F.

Spoon some of the tomato sauce into a casserole dish. Fill each tortilla with a portion of the bean mixture and a bit of cheese. Roll and place seam down in a the casserole baking dish. Spread the remaining tomato sauce evenly over the tortillas. Top with the remaining cheese and oregano. Bake until hot and bubbly, about 20 to 25 minutes.

 Nutritional Information

Per serving: Calories: 438,
Protein: 20 gm., Fat: 11 gm.,
Carbohydrates: 64 gm.

Bob Bland
bland@sover.net
www.sover.net/~bland

Side Dishes

Papas Chorreadas

Yield: 4 to 6 servings

I often skip the Jack cheese to avoid the fat, which gives a soupy result. That can be avoided by using the Jack or skipping the cottage cheese, which still yields a tasty dish.

4 to 6 medium red (or 6 to 8 Russian Banana) potatoes, peeled if desired (about 2-3 pounds)
2 cups or so green beans, fresh or frozen, cut into 1-inch lengths
1 to 2 tablespoons olive oil
1 onion, chopped (about ½ cup)
1 to 2 cloves garlic, minced
1 to 2 jalapeños, minced
1 teaspoon ground cumin
1 teaspoon oregano
3 cups freshly chopped tomatoes, or 1 pint canned
1 cup low-fat cottage cheese (optional)
1 cup Monterey Jack cheese (optional)
½ teaspoon salt
¼ cup fresh cilantro, chopped, or 1 tablespoon dried

Cut the potatoes into 1-inch chunks. Steam them for 15 to 20 minutes until a fork penetrates easily. Add the green beans to the potatoes 2 to 5 minutes before the potatoes are ready, depending on whether the beans are fresh or frozen.

Heat the olive oil in a large (at least 12-inch) skillet. Add the onion, and cook until tender. Add the garlic, jalapeño, cumin, and oregano. Sauté 1 more minute, then add the tomatoes. Simmer on low heat for 10 minutes. Stir in the cottage cheese, mix, and add the Jack cheese, salt, and some cilantro. Heat just until the cheese melts and spreads over the potato/bean mixture.

Bob Bland
bland@sover.net
www.sover.net/~bland

Nutritional Information

Per serving: Calories: 268, Protein: 4 gm., Fat: 4 gm., Carbohydrates: 54 gm.

Potatoes Mendicino

Yield 4 to 6 servings

6 to 8 medium red waxy potatoes, cut into 1-inch chunks (about 3 to 4 cups)

2 medium carrots, sliced ½ inch thick (about 1 cup)

1 to 2 tablespoons olive oil, or ⅓ cup sherry

1 onion, chopped (about ½ cup)

1 to 2 cloves garlic, minced

1 green or red bell pepper, cut into 1-inch squares

½ pound fresh mushrooms, cut into large chunks

2 tablespoons Dijon mustard

2 tablespoons soy sauce

1 cup red wine (optional)

1 to 1½ cups vegetable stock (or potato water), the amount depending on whether using wine

Steam the potatoes and carrots for 15 minutes.

When the potatoes and carrots are almost ready, heat the oil in a 2-quart saucepan, and add the onion. Stir until the onion is translucent. Add the garlic, bell pepper, and mushrooms, and continue to stir.

Sauté until the mushrooms sweat, then add the mustard, soy sauce, red wine, and stock. Stir, then add the potatoes and carrots. Bring to a boil, reduce the heat, cover, and simmer, until tender and well flavored (about 10 minutes). If desired, cook uncovered for up to 10 minutes to reduce and thicken.

Bob Bland
bland@sover.net
www.sover.net/~bland

 Nutritional Information

Per serving: Calories: 355, Protein: 5 gm., Fat: 6 gm., Carbohydrates: 71 gm.

Provençal Potato & Olive Casserole

Yield: 4 to 6 servings

Whether you use white or yellow potatoes gives a much different texture to a potato dish. I grow Yukon Gold, Saginaw Gold, and Granolas for this type of dish. Yellow Finns are a good commercial yellow potato that doesn't do well in my soil. You can also use the generic Maine or Idaho whites, which are almost always Russet Burbanks, production of which represents some 60 percent of US potatoes, a dangerous (not to say boring) monopoly IMHO (in my honest opinion).

2 quarts water
4 to 6 medium white or yellow potatoes (2 to 3 pounds) or other all-purpose type, sliced ¼ inch thick
1 tablespoon olive oil
1 red onion, thinly sliced (just over ½ cup)
½ teaspoon thyme
¼ teaspoon fennel seeds (optional)
¼ teaspoon black pepper
2 tablespoons capers
1 pint canned tomatoes, or 3 cups fresh, chopped
1 to 2 cloves garlic, thinly sliced
½ cup chopped black olives

Bring the water to a boil, add the potatoes, and boil for 3 minutes. Scoop out the potatoes and set aside to drain.

Heat the olive oil in a skillet, and add the onions, thyme, fennel, and black pepper. Sauté until the onions soften, add the capers, and heat for 30 seconds or so. Set aside. Cover the bottom of a 2 to 3-quart baking dish with a thin film of olive oil.

Preheat the oven to 400°F.

Combine all of the ingredients, place in the baking dish, and bake uncovered for 25 minutes.

Variation: Layer the potatoes and tomatoes with cheese (mozzarella, gouda, or fontina), or dot with chevre. Bake at 375°F for 30 minutes or until the cheese is bubbly.

Bob Bland
bland@sover.net
www.sover.net/~bland

 Nutritional Information

Per serving: Calories: 268, Protein: 4 gm., Fat: 5 gm., Carbohydrates: 51 gm.

94

Potato Burritos

Yield: 4 to 6 servings

Another wonderful blend of Mexican cuisine and the potato. I fancy that somehow this ends up as Incan cuisine, but I have never heard a word about either Incan or Peruvian cooking. I have never quite got the technique of making my own tortillas, but a local Vermont company makes wonderful whole wheat ones so I am not inclined to try. Why does Vermont have so many salsa and tortilla makers? The heat keeps us warm all winter!

1 to 2 tablespoons olive oil
3 to 6 all-purpose potatoes, such as Yukon Gold or Katahdin, diced (about 2 cups)
2 teaspoons ground anchos or other chili
1 teaspoon ground cumin
2 medium tomatoes, peeled and diced, or 1 pint canned
6 to 8 scallions, thinly sliced (reserve half for topping)
1 cup grated Monterey Jack cheese (reserve half for topping)
¼ cup chopped, fresh cilantro, or 1 tablespoon dried
1 to 2 jalapeños, minced
½ teaspoon cayenne (optional)
4 to 6 whole wheat tortillas or other flour tortillas

Heat the oil in a skillet over high heat. Add the potatoes and cook until golden, stirring often, about 7 to 8 minutes. Reduce the heat to low. Add the ground chilies and cumin, and cook 2 more minutes. Add the tomatoes and half the scallions. Cover and cook until the potatoes are tender, about 5 minutes. Add half of the Jack cheese, the cilantro, and jalapeños, and stir until the cheese melts. Season with cayenne if desired.

Preheat the oven to 400°F.

Top the tortillas with the potato mix, and roll up. Place seam side down in a baking dish. Sprinkle with the remaining Jack cheese. Cover and bake until heated through and bubbling, about 20 minutes. Top with the remaining scallions.

Bob Bland
bland@sover.net
www.sover.net/~bland

Nutritional Information

Per serving: Calories: 417,
Protein: 11 gm., Fat: 12 gm.,
Carbohydrates: 64 gm.

Crêpes with Asparagus & Sesame Cream Sauce

Yield: 3 to 6 servings

I only eat asparagus when it comes in locally, which makes it a magnificent seasonal treat. Here the asparagus is not cooked or even steamed prior to baking in the crêpes. If you are using asparagus that was not cut on the day of cooking, you may wish to steam it briefly, say 30 seconds to 1 minute. If it is thick supermarket asparagus, steam until it is almost tender. I also make this with wonderful whole wheat tortillas that are locally made, but crêpes are much more traditional.

¼ cup sesame seeds
4 cups skim milk
¼ cup cream of wheat or rice cereal or flour
1 pound pencil thin asparagus spears
12 tortillas or crêpes (see page 88)
2 cups Monterey Jack cheese
½ cup chopped, fresh cilantro, or 2 tablespoons dried
½ teaspoon cayenne

In a saucepan, toast the sesame seeds over moderate heat until golden brown. Pour in the milk and bring to a boil. Stir in the cream cereal or flour, and boil, stirring frequently, until thickened, about 4 to 5 minutes. Remove from the heat and set aside. When cool, whisk until smooth.

Preheat the oven to 400°F.

Place the tortilla or crêpe on a work surface. Sprinkle with a bit of the cheese. Place 4 to 5 asparagus spears on each tortilla, and roll up. Put in a casserole dish, and cover with the sauce. Bake for 8 minutes. Top with cilantro.

Bob Bland
bland@sover.net
www.sover.net/~bland

 Nutritional Information

Per serving: Calories: 531, Protein: 27 gm., Fat: 22 gm., Carbohydrates: 53 gm.

Portobello Stir-Fry

Yield: 4 to 6 servings

I can't believe that nobody turned me onto portobello mushrooms before! Some friends were coming over for dinner, and I stopped off to get something for a stir-fry. The store was out of oyster mushrooms, but there was an unmarked bin with huge mushrooms in it. I flagged down a grocery clerk and asked him what they were. He went in back, came out in a few minutes, and hold me "$4.50 per pound." I explained that I was more interested in what type of mushroom it was. So I picked up two mushrooms and some other odds 'n ends and made a stir-fry, served along with banana squash steamed and mashed with butter and nutmeg, and some leftover Rice With Different Stuff In It (page 86).

1 tablespoon mellow brown rice miso

1 cup warm water

1 tablespoon cornstarch

2 teaspoons soy sauce

⅛ teaspoon Chinese 5-spice powder

1 to 2 tablespoons peanut oil

2 cloves garlic, minced

1 teaspoon fresh ginger, minced

2 portobello mushrooms (about ½ pound), cut into 1 x ½ x ½-inch chunks

1 carrot, sliced ¼ inch thick

½ head broccoli, cut into florets; split the stem and slice ¼ inch thick

1 can sliced water chestnuts

1 medium zucchini, sliced ¼ inch thick

½ pound extra firm tofu, drained and cut into ½-inch cubes

Splash of sake, white wine, or dry sherry

(and/or anything else that seems like a good idea at the time)

Dissolve the miso in the water. Dissolve the cornstarch in a few tablespoons of hot water, and add to the miso along with the soy sauce and 5-spice powder. Set aside.

Heat the wok, then add the peanut oil; heat for a minute and swirl around to coat the wok. Add the garlic and ginger, and stir until the garlic starts to brown.

Add the mushrooms and toss for about 3 minutes until they start to soften. Add the carrot and stir for about 2 minutes, then add the broccoli, and stir for another minute. Add the water chestnuts, stir for another minute, then add the zucchini and tofu. Add a splash of sake, and stir for 1 or 2 more minutes as the steam melds everything. Pour on the sauce. Stir until it thickens (about 3 minutes). Serve with rice or noodles.

As always, "Eat! Eat!"

Chuck Narad

Nutritional Information

Per serving: Calories: 151, Protein: 5 gm., Fat: 6 gm., Carbohydrates: 18 gm.

Portobello Steaks Piccata

Yield: 6 servings

6 large portobello mushrooms,
  sliced ¾ inch thick
Olive oil
Mushroom broth (from baking
  the mushrooms)
½ cup white wine
⅓ cup lemon juice
1 stick butter
1 tablespoon capers

Brush the mushroom slices lightly with the olive oil, and arrange the pieces in a baking dish. Bake uncovered at 350°F for around 20 to 30 minutes until the mushrooms are dark brown and slightly shrunken. Meanwhile, heat the mushroom broth that reduces from the cooked mushrooms, add the white wine, ⅓ cup lemon juice, butter, and capers. Simmer for a few minutes, then pour over the mushrooms just before serving.

If you want, you can thicken the sauce by adding ½ tablespoon arrowroot or cornstarch before heating it. The mushrooms come out very chewy and flavorful, great stuff!

Oh, and I probably slipped in a few cloves of minced garlic on general principles.

Chuck Narad

Nutritional Information

Per serving: Calories: 172,
Protein: 0 gm., Fat: 16 gm.,
Carbohydrates: 3 gm.

Marinated Tofu

Yield: marinade for 1 pound tofu

Ginger Marinade:
½ cup light soy sauce
½ cup dry sherry
2 tablespoons grated, fresh
   gingerroot
2 cloves garlic, minced

Nutritional Information

Per tablespoon: Calories: 15,
Protein: 1 gm., Fat: 0 gm.,
Carbohydrates: 2 gm.

Chili Marinade:
½ cup light soy sauce
½ cup lime juice
1 tablespoon ground cumin
1 tablespoon olive oil
2 serrano chilies, seeded and
   diced

Nutritional Information

Per tablespoon: Calories: 13,
Protein: 1 gm., Fat: 1 gm.,
Carbohydrates: 1 gm.

Orange Marinade:
1 cup orange juice
3 tablespoons Jamaican jerk
   sauce

Nutritional Information

Per tablespoon: Calories: 7,
Protein: 0 gm., Fat: 0 gm.,
Carbohydrates: 2 gm.

The length of time you marinate tofu is pretty much determined by the amount of time you have—the longer, the better. If you plan to marinate it longer than a couple of hours, store it in the refrigerator, especially in warm weather.

To marinate tofu, press it by splitting the block lengthwise. Lay several layers of paper towel on a flat surface. Place the tofu cut side down on the towels, put another couple of layers of paper towel on top, cover with something flat and rigid (I use a cutting board), and place a weight on top (I use a gallon jug of brandy). Let it set for 45 minutes or longer. This presses out the excess water in the tofu and makes it chewier and less likely to crumble. It can then be grilled or baked, or cut up for use in stir-fries. I usually marinate it after pressing. Here are a couple of marinades to get you started.

Chuck Narad

Garlic Mushrooms

Yield: 6 to 8 servings

1 small onion, chopped
1 small mild green chilli, seeds removed and chopped
8 cloves garlic, minced
1 tablespoon olive oil or water
2 pounds mushrooms, roughly chopped
3 tablespoons nutritional yeast flakes
1 teaspoon salt
1 teaspoon black pepper
2 tablespoons tamari or shoyu
¼ cup rich vegetable stock, or 1 teaspoon Vecon (for Brits)
3 tablespoons whole wheat flour
½ cup soya milk

Fry the onion, chilli, and garlic in the oil or water. Add the mushrooms to the pan, cover, and cook over medium heat for about 7 minutes. The mushrooms should reduce, but there should be some liquid in the pan. Add the nutritional yeast flakes, salt, pepper, tamari, and vegetable stock. If there is too much liquid, simmer the mixture for a couple of minutes. In a small bowl or cup, combine the flour and soya milk into a paste. Add the mixture to the mushrooms, stirring quickly to prevent lumps. If the mixture becomes too firm, add a little more soya milk.

Michael Traub
traub@mistral.co.uk

Nutritional Information

Per serving: Calories: 94,
Protein: 5 gm., Fat: 2 gm.,
Carbohydrates: 12 gm.

Moroccan Spinach

Yield: 4 servings

½ cup water
3 cloves garlic, minced
1 large Spanish onion, chopped
½ teaspoon black pepper
2 teaspoons cumin
1 dried red chilli
1 (15-ounce) can chick-peas
   (garbanzo beans)
4 large dried peaches or apricots
1 pound spinach, washed and
   shredded
2 tablespoons tomato purée

Bring the water to a boil in a medium saucepan. Add the garlic, onion, black pepper, and cumin, cover, and simmer for 5 minutes.

Add the dried red chilli and chick-peas. Leave to simmer for about 5 minutes. Cut the dried peaches or apricots into tiny pieces, and add to the pan. Add the spinach and simmer until it reduces down. Add the tomato purée and simmer for another couple of minutes until the mixture has thickened.

Serve over steamed couscous (whole grain is a good choice).

Michael Traub
traub@mistral.co.uk

 Nutritional Information

Per serving: Calories: 238,
Protein: 11 gm., Fat: 2 gm.,
Carbohydrates: 42 gm.

Dal

Yield: Serves 2 hungry people

Here is a version of an Indian staple. A teaspoonful of butter/ghee over each serving enhances the flavor of all the spices.

3 cups water
1⅔ cups dried red or orange
    lentils
1 (16-ounce) can chopped
    tomatoes
2 tablespoons chili powder
2 tablespoons turmeric powder
3 tablespoons butter or ghee
1 large onion, finely sliced
2 tablespoons cumin seeds
5 cloves garlic, finely sliced
1¼ inch gingerroot, finely
    chopped
Salt to taste
Fresh coriander leaves (cilantro),
    chopped

Bring the water to a boil, and add the lentils. Add the tomatoes, chili powder, and turmeric, and simmer for 30 to 45 minutes, or until soft.

In a separate smaller pan, heat the butter, add the onion and cumin seeds, and fry until the onion turns gold. Add the garlic and gingerroot, and fry for 2 more minutes.

Empty the contents of the smaller pan into the larger one, and simmer, stirring for 2 minutes. Add salt to taste. Garnish with the fresh coriander leaves, and serve with steaming hot basmati rice.

Arshiya Noorani

Nutritional Information

Per serving: Calories: 424,
Protein: 15 gm., Fat: 19 gm.,
Carbohydrates: 48 gm.

Potato & Radish Dal

Yield: 6 servings

2 teaspoons cumin
2 teaspoons coriander
1 teaspoon turmeric
2 teaspoons paprika
2 tablespoons vegetable oil
2 fresh green chillies, chopped
3 cloves garlic, crushed
½ inch grated root ginger
  (gingerroot)
1 large Spanish onion, chopped
1 dozen radishes, peeled
2 medium potatoes, cubed
1 (14½-ounce) can chopped
  tomatoes
2 cups dried red lentils
1 teaspoon salt
½ teaspoon black pepper
2 tablespoons tomato purée

Make a masala by sautéing all the spices in the hot oil over medium heat in a large, heavy frying pan or pot. Add the green chillies, garlic, ginger, and onion. Sauté until the spices are well combined and fragrant.

Add the whole radishes and potatoes, and sauté in the masala for a couple of minutes. Add the tomatoes, lentils, salt, and black pepper. Cook until the lentils are pulverized, adding water as necessary to keep the mixture from sticking to the pan. Add the tomato purée and serve with brown rice.

Michael Traub
traub@mistral.co.uk

 Nutritional Information

Per serving: Calories: 388,
Protein: 16 gm., Fat: 5 gm.,
Carbohydrates: 70 gm.

Spanish Rice

Yield: 4 to 6 servings

I presume there is some Spanish dish from which this concept originated, but being unfamiliar with Spanish cuisine, I don't know what it is called. The idea is similar to paella, but without the saffron that is the theme of that dish, so Spanish rice may be simply the result of Americanizing paella.

1 cup uncooked brown rice, preferably long-grain
4 to 6 medium tomatoes, roughly chopped, or 1 pint canned whole tomatoes, chopped

Plus any or all of the following:
2 to 3 cloves garlic, minced
1 medium onion, chopped, (about ½ cup), or 1 small onion, chopped, plus 4 to 5 scallions, sliced
1 green or red bell pepper, chopped
2 jalapeños, minced
½ cup split, small, pitted black olives
½ cup capers, preferably the large Spanish types
1 teaspoon ground cumin
1 tablespoon oregano
1 teaspoon salt
¼ cup chopped, fresh cilantro, or 1 tablespoon dried
1 teaspoon paprika
Pinch saffron or other available spices, herbs, pepper sauce, etc.

Place the rice and tomatoes, plus any of the optional ingredients you choose to use, in a 6-quart pot, and add 2 cups water plus dashes of olive oil and wine or wine vinegar. Bring to a boil, lower the heat, and simmer 45 minutes (checking the moisture occasionally) until the rice is tender and the liquid is mostly absorbed. Serve warm with perhaps a garnish or a sprinkling of cheese.

Bob Bland
bland@sover.net
www.sover.net/~bland

Nutritional Information

Per serving: Calories: 183, Protein: 4 gm., Fat: 4 gm., Carbohydrates: 35 gm.

Michael's Quick & Easy Bulgur

Yield: 6 servings

1 large Spanish onion, chopped
2 cloves garlic, minced
3 tablespoons olive oil
2 cups vegetable stock
2 cups bulgur
1 pound spinach, washed and finely chopped
1 teaspoon salt (use only if stock is unsalted)
½ teaspoon black pepper

Sauté the onion and garlic in the olive oil over medium heat until golden.

Bring the vegetable stock to a boil in a medium saucepan, and add the bulgur, onions, garlic, spinach, salt (if using), and black pepper, and simmer until the bulgur is very tender, about 10 to 15 minutes.

Michael Traub
traub@mistral.co.uk

Nutritional Information

Per serving: Calories: 237,
Protein: 7 gm., Fat: 7 gm.,
Carbohydrates: 36 gm.

Kasha

Yield: 6 to 8 servings

For kasha varnishkes, add 1 to 2 cups of cooked bow-tie noodles before serving.

1 medium onion, chopped
1 clove garlic, minced
1 tablespoon oil
2 eggs
2 cups kasha (cracked
    buckwheat groats)
4 cups water
1 tablespoon miso
½ teaspoon black pepper

Brown the onion and garlic in the oil in the bottom of a medium-sized pot. Beat the eggs loosely, mix thoroughly with the uncooked kasha, and place in a dry pan over medium heat. Stir constantly until the egg coating is dry. Add to the onion, add water, miso, and pepper, and bring to a boil. Immediately cover and reduce the heat to low; the kasha will absorb the water in about 10 minutes and is ready to serve right away.

Chuck Narad

Nutritional Information

Per serving: Calories: 108,
Protein: 3 gm., Fat: 4 gm.,
Carbohydrates: 14 gm.

Quick Rice with Fruit & Nuts

Yield: 4 to 6 servings

1 onion, chopped
2 cloves garlic, minced
1 tablespoon olive oil
1½ cups white basmati rice
3 cups water
Pinch of salt, or 1 vegetable
  bouillon cube
¼ cup black and/or golden
  raisins
¼ cup dried cranberries
  (optional)
¼ cup slivered almonds and/or
  cashews
1 cup chopped mushrooms
½ cup chopped broccoli florets
2 teaspoons curry powder
½ teaspoon turmeric
½ teaspoon cumin
⅛ teaspoon nutmeg
⅛ teaspoon cardamom

Sauté the onion and garlic in the oil in a medium saucepan until soft. Add the rice, water, and salt or bouillon cube, and bring to a boil. Add the raisins, cranberries, almonds or cashews, mushrooms, broccoli, and spices. Stir just enough to combine, cover, reduce the heat to low, and cook for 20 minutes until the rice is done. Halfway through the cooking time, stir briefly again just to mix the mushroom pieces back into the rice.

If you want to use brown basmati rice, increase the cooking time to about 40 minutes.

Chuck Narad

Nutritional Information

Per serving: Calories: 248,
Protein: 5 gm., Fat: 7 gm.,
Carbohydrates: 41 gm.

Fried Rice

Yield: 4 to 6 servings

1 cup uncooked rice (calrose or basmati)
1 can bamboo shoots
1 cup bean sprouts
3 to 6 scallions, finely chopped
1 can water chestnuts, coarsely chopped
1 egg (omit for vegan)
Large handful of snow peas, stems removed
4 cloves garlic, minced
1 tablespoon minced fresh gingerroot
¼ cup light soy sauce
1 tablespoon wine vinegar
White pepper to taste
¼ cup peanut oil (or a little less)

Cook the rice while preparing the vegetables by bringing it to a boil in 2 cups of water, stirring briefly, covering, and reducing the heat to low. Keep covered (don't peek) for 18 minutes—then fluff with a fork. Heat the wok, beat the egg with a splash of water, scramble the egg, chop it up, and set it aside.

Put the oil in the wok, and let it heat. Add the garlic and ginger, stir-fry for 1 minute, then add the cooked rice. Stir and toss for about 3 minutes. Then add (1 minute apart) the bamboo shoots, water chestnuts, snow peas, bean sprouts, and scallions. Stir-fry for about 2 minutes, then add the egg, soy sauce, and vinegar; stir to mix. Sprinkle with white pepper (about ¼ teaspoon or to taste).

Chuck Narad

 Nutritional Information

Per serving: Calories: 264, Protein: 6 gm., Fat: 12 gm., Carbohydrates: 32 gm.

Bhindi Bhaji

Yield: 4 to 6 servings

1 large Spanish onion, finely
  chopped
2 cloves garlic, minced
½ teaspoon turmeric
1 teaspoon black mustard seeds
  plus 3 tablespoons vegetable
  oil
1 fresh red chilli, seeds removed
  and chopped, or 1 teaspoon
  cayenne pepper
1 tablespoon tomato purée or
  paste
½ cup water
1 pound baby okra
Salt to taste

Fry the onion, garlic, turmeric, mustard seeds, and red chilli in the oil. Add the tomato purée and water, and cook until well mixed and thickened. Add the whole okra and simmer for about 15 minutes. Add salt if necessary. Serve over rice.

Michael Traub
traub@mistral.co.uk

 Nutritional Information

Per serving: Calories: 48,
Protein: 2 gm., Fat: 0 gm.,
Carbohydrates: 10 gm.

Broiled Marinated Vegetables

Yield: 8 servings

2 pounds mixed baby squash (zucchini, yellow squash, pattypan, crookneck), split lengthwise

4 baby Japanese eggplant, sliced into thirds lengthwise

¼ cup olive oil

1 cup light soy sauce

1 cup lime juice

2 tablespoons minced, fresh gingerroot

6 cloves garlic, minced

2 tablespoons ground cumin seed

Combine all the ingredients in a large bowl, and marinate for 1 to 2 hours. Spread the vegetables out in a flat casserole dish, cover with the marinade, and broil for about 10 minutes. Scoop out of the dish, and serve.

Note: Any part that is not covered with marinade will char. The leftover marinade makes a good stir-fry sauce or gravy over rice.

You can also marinate the vegetables overnight, then grill them on an outdoor barbeque in a grilling basket.

Chuck Narad

 Nutritional Information

Per serving: Calories: 135, Protein: 5 gm., Fat: 7 gm., Carbohydrates: 14 gm.

Aloo Gobi (sorta)

Yield: 4 to 6 servings

2 tablespoons olive oil or ghee
½ teaspoon ground allspice
1 tablespoon cumin powder
1 medium onion, chopped
3 cloves garlic, minced
White wine
¼ cup sunflower seeds
2 tablespoons minced, fresh
  gingerroot
2 potatoes, peeled and cut into
  large cubes
½ head of cauliflower, separated
  into florets
¼ cup raisins
1 head of broccoli, separated
  into florets and stems (stems
  split and sliced)
¼ cup roasted red peppers
½ teaspoon salt
½ teaspoon black pepper
½ teaspoon cayenne
Water

Heat the olive oil in a deep pan at medium-high. Add the allspice and cumin.

Sauté the onion and garlic until soft. Add some white wine, the sunflower seeds, and the ginger-root, and stir regularly. As the wine boils off, add a little more; alternate between a splash of wine and a splash of water throughout the cooking. Make sure that the cook gets only wine internally.

Next, add the potatoes and more liquid; keep stirring. After about 5 to 10 minutes, add the cauliflower and raisins; after 10 minutes more add the broccoli and red peppers. Keep stirring and keep adding liquids. When the broccoli is soft, add the salt, black pepper, and cayenne.

Serve with Dal (page 102) over basmati rice and a side of yogurt and some chapatis or tortillas.

Chuck Narad

 Nutritional Information

Per serving: Calories: 204,
Protein: 4 gm., Fat: 9 gm.,
Carbohydrates: 26 gm.

Vegetable Potstickers

Yield: 24 potstickers (8 to 10 servings)

These vegetarian potstickers are steamed rather than cooked in oil. Serve with Easy Dipping Sauce (on next page).

Dough:
1 tablespoon active dry yeast
½ cup warm water
2 tablespoons nonfat dry milk
2 tablespoons honey
1 cup whole wheat flour
⅛ teaspoon salt
About ¾ cup unbleached flour

Filling:
3 cloves garlic, minced
1 tablespoon grated, fresh
    gingerroot
1 tablespoon oil
1 cup chopped mushrooms
    (about ¼ pound)
2 medium carrots, diced
1 cup chopped mung bean
    sprouts
2 tablespoons tamari or soy
    sauce
1 teaspoon sesame oil
3 scallions, thinly sliced
2 tablespoons cornstarch
    dissolved in 2 tablespoons
    water
1 cup vegetable broth or water
    for steaming

To make the dough, dissolve the yeast in the warm water, and let set for 10 minutes, or until bubbly. Add the milk, honey, whole wheat flour, and salt, and beat well. Stir in enough unbleached flour to make a firm dough. Knead for 5 minutes or until the dough is smooth and elastic. Cover and let rise in a warm place until doubled, about 1½ hours. Punch down, cover, and let rest another 15 minutes or until ready to shape.

To make the filling, sauté the garlic and gingerroot in 1 tablespoon oil in a wok or large skillet for 1 minute over medium-high heat. Add the mushrooms, carrots, and mung bean sprouts, and cook 2 more minutes. Add the tamari and sesame oil, and cook until thickened. Cover and let cool to room temperature.

Divide the dough into 24 balls. On a floured board, roll each ball into a 3 to 4-inch circle. Fill each circle with 1 heaping teaspoon of filling. Fold and crimp edges to form half-moon shaped potstickers. Cover until ready to steam.

Spray a nonstick wok or large skillet with vegetable cooking spray. Heat over medium-high. Put half of the potstickers seam-

 Nutritional Information

Per serving: Calories: 142,
Protein: 5 gm., Fat: 2 gm.,
Carbohydrates: 26 gm.

side down in the wok, add ½ cup of the broth or water, cover, and steam for 6 minutes or until the wok is dry. Uncover and continue to cook until the potstickers are starting to brown, turning if needed. Repeat with the second batch. Serve with Easy Dipping Sauce.

Nanette Blanchard
76702.3406@compuserve.com

Easy Dipping Sauce

Yield: ½ cup

Use this versatile sauce for dipping potstickers, egg rolls, and won ton.

¼ cup tamari or soy sauce
¼ cup balsamic vinegar
4 scallions, thinly sliced

Mix all the ingredients and serve at room temperature.

Nanette Blanchard
76702.3406@compuserve.com

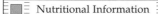 Nutritional Information

Per tablespoon: Calories: 9,
Protein: 1 gm., Fat: 0 gm.,
Carbohydrates: 1 gm.

Baigan Bharta

Yield: 6 servings

1 medium eggplant
2 tablespoons ghee or
  vegetable oil
2 to 3 serrano chilies, seeded
  and diced
¼ teaspoon compound
  asafetida* (or ⅛ teaspoon
  pure)
1 to 2 teaspoons cumin seeds
2 teaspoons ground coriander
1 teaspoon salt
2 tablespoons chopped, fresh
  cilantro
⅔ cup nonfat yogurt
1 to 2 teaspoons garam masala*

*Pungent Indian spices you can find in
 Asian groceries or specialty food
 stores. See also page 33.*

Bake the eggplant 40 minutes at 425°F on a baking sheet. Split it and scoop out the pulp; discard the skin.

Heat the ghee on medium; add cumin seeds, serranos, and asafetida. Cook until the cumin seeds darken. Add the eggplant, salt, and coriander; cook for about 10 minutes, stirring occasionally. When it thickens, remove from the heat, add the yogurt, cilantro, and garam masala, and serve. (The yogurt might curdle; to prevent that, let the eggplant cool first, then add the yogurt, etc., then briefly reheat.)

Chuck Narad

Nutritional Information

Per serving: Calories: 82,
Protein: 2 gm., Fat: 5 gm.,
Carbohydrates: 7 gm.

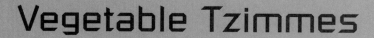

Vegetable Tzimmes

Yield: about 12 servings

ed.—A wonderfully aromatic dish to prepare when the weather is cold and dreary and you have a lazy weekend day to tend to something in the kitchen.

4 sweet potatoes, peeled and diced into 1½-inch chunks
1 pound carrots, peeled and sliced ¼ inch thick
1 medium Spanish onion, quartered and thinly sliced
1 cup dried apricots
¾ cup raisins
Water
2 tablespoons vegetable bouillon
¼ cup honey
Salt and pepper to taste
½ cup butter
2 tablespoons flour

To a large cooking pot, add the sweet potatoes, carrots, onion, apricots, and raisins. Fill the pot about ¾ full with water, to just above the vegetables. Add the bouillon and honey, season with the salt and pepper, and mix well. Bake at 350°F for 1½ hours.

Remove from the oven. Melt the butter in a saucepan, add the flour, and stir until very lightly browned. Add 1½ cups of the cooking liquid, stirring slowly to make a sauce. Stir the sauce into the cooking pot. Turn down the oven to 225°F, and bake again for about 20 minutes until well thickened.

Paul Walters
pwal@interaccess.com

 Nutritional Information

Per serving: Calories: 250,
Protein: 2 gm., Fat: 7 gm.,
Carbohydrates: 42 gm.

Winter Squash Bake

Yield: 8 servings

ed.—Here's a delicious new twist to Thanksgiving squash and cranberries that's bound to become a new tradition at your house.

1 winter squash: acorn, butternut, turban, etc. (If you use acorn squash, you may need two small ones.)
2 medium sweet potatoes
2 medium cooking apples (Cortland, Rome, etc.)
¾ cup raisins
1 cup cranberries
1 (18-ounce) can vegetable broth, or 1½ cups homemade broth, or 1½ cups hot water plus 2 tablespoons powered vegetable bouillon

Peel the squash, sweet potatoes, and apples. Halve the squash and remove the seeds. Core the apples.

Cut the squash, potatoes, and apples into 1-inch chunks. Combine the broth with salt, freshly ground black pepper, and 2 teaspoons curry powder. Mix all the ingredients in a large casserole or baking dish. Bake at 300°F for 50 to 60 minutes, or until the vegetables are tender.

Depending on the vegetables and apples, this may need to be thickened. To do so, mix 2 tablespoons flour with ½ cup water to form a light roux, place the casserole on a low burner until it reaches a light boil, and mix in the roux, stirring until the broth thickens.

Paul Walters
pwal@interaccess.com

 Nutritional Information

Per serving: Calories: 152, Protein: 2 gm., Fat: 0 gm., Carbohydrates: 35 gm.

Polenta

Yield: 4 to 6 servings

I had always thought of polenta as just being wet corn bread and could never get excited about the concept. And then I had some at one of the wonderful restaurants tucked back in the Vermont hills. Wow! Thinking of polenta as corn bread is like thinking of pasta as flour paste. And like pasta, polenta can be served with thousands of sauces. Stone ground cornmeal is best, and the nature of the corn will make a difference. Don't try it with ordinary supermarket cornmeal or you will not get the true experience.

4 cups water
1 generous cup stone ground cornmeal
1 teaspoon salt
2 tablespoons butter, cut into bits
4 tablespoons grated Parmesan

Bring the water to a boil in a saucepan. Over low heat, drizzle in the cornmeal very slowly, whisking continuously with a wire whisk. During the process, add the salt. Continue to whisk the polenta until a thick mass develops, then switch to a wooden spoon. Stir continuously until the polenta hardly comes off the spoon, about 5 to 7 minutes. Add the Parmesan and butter, and stir another minute or two.

Serve as pudding-like mounds topped by a sauce. The polenta will "set" as it cools. If not prepared to serve immediately, divide into servings, and let set before covering with sauce.

Serve with almost any sauce used for heavier pastas, such as putanesca, fresca, puglia, or even just olive oil in which garlic has been lightly browned.

Bob Bland
bland@sover.net
www.sover.net/~bland

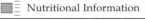
Nutritional Information

Per serving: Calories: 162, Protein: 4 gm., Fat: 7 gm., Carbohydrates: 22 gm.

Rice & Barley Pilaf

Yield: 6 servings

¾ cup brown rice
¾ cup pearled barley
3¾ to 4 cups water
1 medium carrot, cut in small
  dice
¾ cup corn, frozen but not
  thawed
1 tablespoon nutritional yeast
1 tablespoon vegetarian chicken-
  style bouillon
1 medium onion, minced
3 cloves garlic, minced
1 stalk celery, chopped
2 tablespoons soy sauce
Ground ginger to taste
1 tablespoon dried parsley
1 teaspoon marjoram
¾ cup peas, frozen but not
  thawed

Place all of the ingredients, except the frozen peas, in a large saucepan. Bring to a boil, lower the heat, cover, and simmer until the grains are tender, about 45 minutes. Add a little more water if needed to cook the grains to your liking. Stir in the frozen peas 5 minutes before the grains are done.

Reggie Dwork
reggie@netcom.com

Nutritional Information

Per serving: Calories: 143,
Protein: 4 gm., Fat: 0 gm.,
Carbohydrates: 3 gm.

Breads

Five-Seed Bread 120

Almond Poppy Seed Bread 122

Killer Garlic Bread 123

Yellow Corn Blueberry Muffins 124

Cheese Scones 125

Wholemeal Scones 126

Banana Bread 127

Corn Muffins 128

Five-Seed Bread

Yield: 8 servings

This yeasted bread is delicious with either sweet or savory sandwich fillings and makes for outstanding PB&Js or great Sunday brunch toast.

1½ tablespoons honey or rice syrup

¾ cup warm water

1 packet dry baking yeast

2 to 3 cups whole wheat flour (or substitute part unbleached flour)

1 teaspoon salt

¼ cup wheat germ

¼ cup cracked wheat, wheat sprouts, or cooked grains

2 tablespoons vital wheat gluten (optional—aids in tenderness of dough)

2 tablespoons caraway seeds

1 tablespoon poppy seeds

1 tablespoon sesame seeds

1 teaspoon celery seeds

½ tablespoon anise seeds

1 tablespoon soy margarine at room temperature (plus more for greasing pan)

2 tablespoons barley malt, honey, or rice syrup

water or oil to brush top of bread loaf

Dissolve the honey in the warm water (about 120°F), and gradually stir in the baking yeast. Set aside.

In a large bowl, blend together 2 cups of the flour with the salt, wheat germ, cracked wheat, wheat gluten, and seeds. Make a well in the center of the flour mixture. When the yeast is foamy, pour it into the well, along with 1 tablespoon soy margarine and the barley malt. Mix with a wooden spoon as much as possible, then turn out onto a floured surface, and let the dough rest for a few minutes while you wash and grease the bowl. Knead the dough for 10 to 15 minutes, adding flour liberally to reduce stickiness. When the dough is very flexible and fairly soft, roll into a ball, and place it in the greased bowl. Cover with a towel or plastic wrap, and set in a warm place to let rise for about an hour until doubled in size.

Gently deflate by kneading the dough, return to the floured surface, and form into a loaf. Place in a greased 8½ x 4½-inch loaf pan or on a greased cookie sheet. Cover with a towel and set aside to rise for about 40 minutes.

 Nutritional Information

Per serving: Calories: 205, Protein: 8 gm., Fat: 2 gm., Carbohydrates: 36 gm.

Preheat the oven to 375°F. Brush the top of the loaf with water or oil, and place in the center of the oven. Bake for 45 minutes, rotating the pan once halfway through. Test for doneness by rapping the bottom of the loaf with your knuckles. If you hear a "hollow" sound, your bread is done (this is a common and hard-to-describe test!). Immediately set on a wire rack to cool thoroughly.

Janet Ingraham
jingraha@freenet.columbus.oh.us

Almond Poppy Seed Bread

Yield: 1 loaf (16 slices)

This is called a "bread" but it has the consistency and yumminess of a cake. Works great as muffins too. Bake muffins for approximately 35 minutes.

3 cups flour
½ teaspoon salt
2 tablespoons poppy seeds
1½ teaspoons baking powder
2½ cups sugar
1½ cups milk
1 cup oil
3 eggs
1½ teaspoons vanilla
2 teaspoons almond extract

Preheat the oven to 350°F.

Mix together the flour, salt, poppy seeds, baking powder, and sugar. In a separate bowl, mix the milk, oil, eggs, vanilla, and almond extract. Pour the wet ingredients into the dry ingredients, and mix well. Pour into a well greased loaf pan (this bread tends to stick).

Bake for approximately 55 minutes.

Wayne Riggs
riggs@email.unc.edu

 Nutritional Information

Per slice: Calories: 388,
Protein: 5 gm., Fat: 16 gm.,
Carbohydrates: 44 gm.

Killer Garlic Bread

Yield: 1 loaf (16 slices)

6 tablespoons butter or margarine

1 *head* of garlic, minced (This is not a typo!—use the entire bulb.)

2 tablespoons Italian spice mix, or a mixture of dried oregano, basil, and marjoram.

¼ cup freshly grated Parmesan cheese

1 loaf *extra sour* sourdough French bread

Peel, smash, and mince a whole head of garlic.

Melt the margarine or butter.

Mix the garlic, Italian spice mix, and grated Parmesan in with the margarine. Split a loaf of sourdough French bread lengthwise, and cover the halves with the vampire-repellent paste. Place on foil or a cookie sheet, and broil until brown. Slice and serve.

This garlic bread repels vampires, insurance salesmen, and door-to-door religious types. (The only drawback is that your clothing smells like garlic for about two weeks.)

Chuck Narad

 Nutritional Information

Per slice: Calories: 159, Protein: 4 gm., Fat: 10 gm., Carbohydrates: 13 gm.

Yellow Corn Blueberry Muffins

Yield: 6 very large muffins or 12 to 15 small muffins

Dry ingredients:
1¼ cups finely ground yellow or blue corn
¾ cup whole wheat pastry flour
½ cup unbleached white flour
½ cup brown rice flour
1 tablespoon baking powder
¼ teaspoon sea salt

Wet ingredients:
¼ pound tofu
⅓ cup canola or corn oil
⅔ cup vanilla or plain soymilk, or replace 1 tablespoon of the soymilk with 1 tablespoon almond butter
¼ cup rice syrup
¼ cup maple syrup

Fruit ingredients:
½ cup blueberries (also good with cherries, cranberries, etc.)

Preheat the oven to 350°F.

Combine and mix all of the dry ingredients. Put the tofu in a blender or a food processor with the oil and enough of the soy milk to blend to a creamy consistency. Add the rest of the wet ingredients to the blender or food processor, and blend. Lightly oil your muffin tin(s), or use muffin cups. Form a well in the middle of the dry ingredients, and pour the wet ingredients into the dry. Fold the wet and the dry together to combine by bringing your spatula underneath the dry and coming up and around. If you stir the batter too vigorously, you will develop the gluten in your flour and your muffins will not cook correctly, so please gently fold your ingredients. When the dry has almost completely absorbed all of the wet, add the blueberries. Fold to complete your mix.

Place the dough into muffin tin wells with 2 spoons. Distribute the batter evenly. If you are making 6 big muffins, do not be afraid to pile them high. Bake the muffins for 40 minutes, then check them. The muffins are done when an inserted toothpick has dry pieces (not gooey) stuck to it. If the toothpick is gooey, then bake for another 5 minutes, and check again. Remove from the oven and let cool for 20 minutes. Eat.

Eric Pierce
epierce@s-cwis.unomaha.edu

 Nutritional Information

Per serving (12): Calories: 215, Protein: 4 gm., Fat: 7 gm., Carbohydrates: 35 gm.

Cheese Scones

Yield: 8 servings

This is nice with cream cheese which has been blended with salsa. Best served warm.

Dry ingredients:
2 cups whole wheat flour
2 teaspoons baking powder
Generous dash cayenne pepper
¼ teaspoon garlic powder
¼ teaspoon chili powder
1⅓ cups grated cheddar cheese
3 tablespoons Parmesan
5 tablespoons chilled margarine

Wet ingredients:
¼ cup salsa
¼ cup milk
2 eggs or equivalent egg
    replacer

Preheat the oven to 400°F, and lightly grease a baking sheet. In a large bowl, stir together the dry ingredients, spices, and cheeses. Cut in the margarine until the mixture has the consistency of coarse crumbs. Stir together the liquid ingredients, including the eggs. Add the liquid ingredients to the dry ingredients, and stir until combined to make a soft dough. You may need to add another couple of tablespoons of water or milk depending on the flour you use. Pat the dough into an 8-inch circle on the baking sheet. Cut into 8 wedges. Bake about 25 minutes until lightly browned and a toothpick inserted into the center of the wedges comes out clean.

Ruth Fink-Winter
wfink@iastate.edu

 Nutritional Information

Per serving: Calories: 274,
Protein: 12 gm., Fat: 16 gm.,
Carbohydrates: 21 gm.

Wholemeal Scones

Yield: 8 to 10 servings

This is my wife's recipe for vegan scones.

1⅔ cups wholemeal (whole wheat) flour

1½ teaspoons baking powder (the amount depends on how fluffy you want them)

½ cup vegan margarine

¼ teaspoon salt

2 teaspoons demerara or other unrefined sugar, or to taste

¾ cup currants or raisins, or to taste

6 to 8 tablespoons soya milk (to bind and glaze)

Sesame seeds for topping

Preheat the oven to 450°F (220°C). Mix the flour and baking powder together, and cut in the margarine until the combined mixture is crumbly. Add the salt, sugar, and currants, and mix well. Mix in enough soya milk with a spoon until a stiff dough is formed, making sure that it is stiff enough that it doesn't stick to the sides of the bowl. Turn out onto a lightly floured board, and knead for about 1 minute. Shape into scones (such as rounds) approximately ½ inch thick. Glaze with a little more soya milk, and top with sesame seeds. Bake for 15 minutes on a greased baking pan or on silicon paper.

For a variation, replace the sugar and currants with 2 cloves of minced garlic and some dried herbs. For a more sour flavour, use soya yogurt in place of the soya milk.

Serve fruit scones with vegan margarine and jam; serve the herb scones just with vegan margarine.

Michael Traub
traub@mistral.co.uk

 Nutritional Information

Per serving: Calories: 218, Protein: 4 gm., Fat: 12 gm., Carbohydrates: 25 gm.

Banana Bread

Yield: 12 to 16 slices

This is the recipe I like to use to make good-for-you banana bread. There's room for adjustments in it if you like.

ed.—And this is a remarkably good banana bread—my kids don't even realize they're eating all these healthful ingredients!

¾ cup whole wheat flour
¾ cup soy flour
2 tablespoons toasted wheat germ
2 tablespoons powdered walnuts (optional)
2¼ teaspoons baking powder
½ teaspoon salt
¾ teaspoon lemon rind, grated (optional)
1 large egg, beaten
¼ cup oil (safflower, walnut, or other good tasting oil)
⅓ cup honey
¼ teaspoon vanilla
1 to 1¼ cups mashed ripe bananas (about 3)
¼ cup chopped walnuts

Preheat the oven to 350°F.

Stir together the wheat flour, soy flour, wheat germ, walnuts, baking powder, salt, and lemon rind.

In another bowl, mix the egg, oil, honey, vanilla, and bananas.

Mix the wet ingredients into the dry ingredients until barely blended. Over-mixing will make the bread tough. Fold in the walnuts.

Bake in a greased 8½ x 4½-inch loaf pan for 45 to 50 minutes. Mmmmmmmmmmm.

Wendy Swanbeck

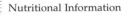
Nutritional Information

Per serving: Calories: 152,
Protein: 4 gm., Fat: 7 gm.,
Carbohydrates: 18 gm.

Corn Muffins

Yield: 12 muffins

1 cup all-purpose flour
1 cup yellow cornmeal
⅓ cup granulated sugar
1 tablespoon baking powder
1 cup cream-style corn
½ cup mayonnaise (can be
  nonfat and/or nondairy)
1 egg white or the equivalent in
  egg replacer
¼ teaspoon salt (optional)

Preheat the oven to 400°F.

In a large bowl, combine the flour, cornmeal, sugar, and baking powder. Make a well in the center of the bowl, and add the corn, mayonnaise, and egg white. Stir just until mixed; do not overbeat. The batter shouldn't be too lumpy, but it's better to leave a few small lumps than to beat out the foam from the baking powder.

Oil a 12-cup muffin pan or use a nonfat cooking spray. Two 6-cup pans can be used, as well as non-stick pans. Divide the batter among the muffin cups, and bake for 20 minutes, or until the tops just begin to brown.

These are very good warm, and they keep well too. They actually gain flavor overnight!

Susan Weinstein
Huntington, W. Va.

 Nutritional Information

Per serving: Calories: 135, Protein: 2 gm., Fat: 2 gm., Carbohydrates: 25 gm.

Desserts

Berry Ice Cream

Yield: approximately 1 litre (4 servings)

I've been experimenting around with ice cream recipes, and as I found a nice selection of frozen berries in my local supermarket recently, I decided that berry ice cream would be a good idea. Normally I have access to a blender, and purée my fruit that way for ice cream. This time I had no blender, so I invented my own method for puréeing the fruit. I think it was a good idea. The resulting ice cream was absolutely delicious!

¼ teaspoon salt
10 fluid ounces double (heavy) cream
5 rounded tablespoons sugar (caster/superfine is best)
4 cups (about 1 pound, 2 ounces) mixed summer fruits (bilberries, strawberries, morello cherries, black currants, raspberries, red currants, blackberries—fresh or frozen)
½ cup water

In a freezer-proof container (at least 1 litre capacity), mix the salt, cream, and 2 rounded tablespoons of the sugar. Put into the freezer to chill.

Meanwhile, put the berries in a pan with the water and the remaining 3 tablespoons of sugar. Heat gently for 10 minutes, stirring frequently until the fruit softens. Let the mixture simmer gently for 15 to 20 minutes, stirring occasionally, so that some of the water can evaporate off. Remove the pan from the heat. The fruit should now be in an unrecognizable mushy state. Using a potato-masher, mash the fruit gently to make sure the mixture has no large lumps of fruit in it. Let the fruit mixture cool.

Remove the cream mixture from the freezer, add the berry mixture, and mix well. Check the mixture for sweetness, add more sugar to taste, and mix well.

Return the container to the freezer, and let the ice-cream freeze. When it is half-frozen (about 4 hours, depending on your freezer), take out the container, beat the ice-cream thoroughly with a fork or whip in a food processor, and return it to the freezer.

Once it is frozen, you should be able to scoop the ice-cream as soon as it is removed from the freezer. If not, remove the container from the freezer 15 minutes before serving.

Sharon.Curtis
sharon.curtis@comlab.oxford.ac.uk

Nutritional Information

Per serving: Calories: 361, Protein: 2 gm., Fat: 26 gm., Carbohydrates: 26 gm.

English-Style Chocolate Chip Cookies

Yield: approximately 4 dozen (1-inch) balls

These biscuits are popular with all my friends. It's good the recipe makes plenty because they don't last long! If you're interested in the origin of the recipe, a friend of my Mum's once bought a packet of biscuits in Cornwall, and they had the recipe on the back. She gave the recipe to me—it was for cherry biscuits and wasn't very good. I have much mutated and improved the original recipe to produce the following treat.

1 cup margarine

1 cup sugar (caster/superfine is best)

2 tablespoons golden syrup or corn syrup

3¾ cups all-purpose flour (1 pound)

1 tablespoon baking powder

12 ounces (at least) of chopped-up chocolate or packets of chocolate chips in white, milk, plain (dark), or a combination

Preheat the oven to 425°F (220°C, GM.7). Lightly grease 2 baking trays.

Mix the margarine, sugar, and syrup well in a large bowl. Combine the flour, baking powder, and chocolate chips, then mix thoroughly with the wet ingredients. The dough should be slightly crumbly and just hold together when you squeeze it. Press walnut-sized balls onto the baking trays, and bake for 8 minutes until they just start to turn brown.

Sharon Curtis
sharon.curtis@comlab.oxford.ac.uk

Nutritional Information

Per cookie: Calories: 115, Protein: 1 gm., Fat: 6 gm., Carbohydrates: 14 gm.

Bird Poop Cookies

Yield: 15 (2-inch) cookies

ed.—Your kids will enjoy these as much for the name as the delicious flavor.

Dry Ingredients:
- 1 cup plus 2 tablespoons whole wheat pastry flour
- ½ cup roasted or raw carob powder
- ½ cup rolled oats
- ½ teaspoon baking powder
- ¼ teaspoon sea salt
- ¼ cup uncooked millet, washed and drained

Wet Ingredients:
- 3 tablespoons canola oil
- ¼ cup soymilk (any variety is fine)
- 3 tablespoons rice syrup
- 3 tablespoons maple syrup
- ¼ cup + 2 tablespoons tahini (sesame butter)
- ½ teaspoon vanilla

Preheat the oven to 350°F.

Combine and mix all of the dry ingredients, except the millet, in a mixing bowl. In a separate bowl, combine and mix all of the wet ingredients. Form a well in the middle of the dry ingredients, and pour the wet ingredients into the dry. Fold (bring your spatula underneath the dry and come up and around) the wet and the dry together to mix. If you stir the batter too vigorously, you will develop the gluten in your flour and your cookies will not cook correctly, so please gently fold your ingredients. When the dry has almost completely absorbed all of the wet, add the millet. Fold to complete your mix. Lightly brush your cookie sheet with oil. Drop 2-inch dough pieces onto your cookie sheet. You may shape your dough with wet fingers if you like. Bake for approximately 26 minutes. Cookies are finished baking when they spring back when you lightly push them. Let cool for 10 minutes. Eat.

Variations: Try using peanut butter instead of tahini.

Eric Pierce
epierce@s-cwis.unomaha.edu

 Nutritional Information

Per 2 cookies: Calories: 159, Protein: 3 gm., Fat: 6 gm., Carbohydrates: 22 gm.

Michael's Low-Fat Date & Banana Cake

Yield: 9 servings

3 cups whole wheat flour
2 tablespoons baking powder
6 dates, pitted and chopped
3 bananas
2 tablespoons rice or corn syrup
1 tablespoon barley malt extract
½ cup applesauce
1 tablespoon vanilla
¼ cup water
¼ cup soya milk
12 whole almonds (optional)

Mix the flour, baking powder, and dates. Combine the bananas, syrup, malt extract, applesauce, vanilla, water, and soya milk in a blender for about 20 seconds. You don't really want the bananas to be totally pulverized; a few little chunks are nice. Mix the liquid and dry ingredients together. Place in an 8-inch baking tin which has been previously coated with nonfat spray and dusted with flour. You can place a few almonds on top of the cake for decoration. Spraying the top of the cake with a little soya milk will help it get more crusty, if you like. Bake at 350°F (180°C) for approximately 1 hour, or until a knife inserted in the middle comes out clean.

This makes dense cake. To make a lighter cake, use a flour with less bran in it, and use concentrated apple juice as a sweetener instead of barley malt extract.

Michael Traub
traub@mistral.co.uk

Nutritional Information

Per serving: Calories: 206,
Protein: 6 gm., Fat: 1 gm.,
Carbohydrates: 43 gm.

Carrot Cake

Yield: 9 servings

1 teaspoon flax seeds
1 cup vegetable oil
1 cup unrefined sugar
¼ cup apple juice
½ cup soya milk
1½ cups unbleached flour
½ cup wholemeal (whole wheat) flour
1 teaspoon baking powder
1 teaspoon baking soda
½ teaspoon salt
½ teaspoon cinnamon
¼ teaspoon ginger
¼ teaspoon nutmeg
4 medium carrots, grated (3 cups)
½ cup raisins
½ cup chopped nuts (optional)

Preheat the oven to 350°F (180°C).

Grind the flax seeds in a blender. Add the oil, sugar, apple juice, and soya milk, and blend until a smooth mixture is formed. Sift the flour into a bowl, and add the baking powder, baking soda, salt, and spices. Pour in the blended mixture, and combine. Add the carrots, raisins, and nuts. Fold the entire mixture together. Pour into a greased and floured 9-inch square baking tin, and cook for about 45 minutes. (A knife inserted into the very center of the cake should come out clean.)

The only problem with this recipe is that the sweetness of the cake is a bit of an unknown until you get it out of the oven and taste it. Sweet carrots make all the difference. You can add more sweetener to the above recipe if you like your cakes quite sweet.

Michael Traub
traub@mistral.co.uk

 Nutritional Information

Per serving: Calories: 431, Protein: 4 gm., Fat: 24 gm., Carbohydrates: 49 gm.

Lokshen Kugel
(Noodle Pudding)

Yield: 6 to 8 servings

Kugels (puddings) are a mainstay in traditional Jewish cooking. Here's one made with egg noodles (lokshen) that is my favorite.

3 eggs
¼ cup brown sugar
1 tablespoon lemon juice
½ cup mixed dark and golden raisins (more to taste)
½ cup slivered almonds
⅛ teaspoon nutmeg
3 tablespoons melted butter or margarine
4 cups cooked wide egg noodles
Bread crumbs for topping

Preheat the oven to 375°F.

Beat the eggs and brown sugar together. Add the lemon juice, raisins, almonds, nutmeg, and butter, and mix well. Combine the mixture with the noodles, and pour into a well-greased baking pan (8 x 8 inches for thick kugel, 8 x 12 inches for thinner). Sprinkle the bread crumbs on top. Bake for 45 to 50 minutes for the 8 x 8-inch pan, 20 minutes for an 8 x 12-inch pan until the top is golden brown. This can be served warm but is delicious cold too. Warning: this stuff is addictive.

Chuck Narad

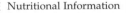

Nutritional Information

Per serving: Calories: 306,
Protein: 9 gm., Fat: 13 gm.,
Carbohydrates: 36 gm.

Passover Candy
(or anytime!)

Yield: about 2 to 3 dozen pieces of candy

My friends will not celebrate Passover unless they have my candy on hand. The ingredients sound a bit odd at first, but wait until you try it! This freezes exceptionally well, so keep some on hand for a midnight snack.

½ cup butter
1 cup slivered almonds
1½ (12-ounce) bags of semi-sweet chocolate bits
2 cups matzo farfel or crushed whole matzo

Cover two cookie sheets with waxed paper, and spray lightly with vegetable oil spray.

In a large saucepan, melt the butter over medium heat. Add the almonds. Stir until the almonds are toasty. (This happens quickly; don't overcook.) Remove the almonds and set aside. Place the chocolate in the saucepan over low heat, and stir until melted (don't overcook). Remove from the heat, and add the almonds and farfel. Stir until everything is well coated. Drop the mixture onto the cookie sheet to form 1½-inch pieces (or however large you like). Put the cookie sheets into the refrigerator, and cool for an hour. Indulge!

Paul Walters
pwal@interaccess.com

Nutritional Information

Per piece: Calories: 161,
Protein: 2 gm., Fat: 11 gm.,
Carbohydrates: 14 gm.

Blueberry Decadents

Yield: 2½ dozen cookies

8 ounces chopped semi-sweet chocolate

¼ cup all-purpose flour
¼ cup cocoa powder
1½ teaspoons cinnamon
¼ teaspoons baking powder
Pinch of salt

6 tablespoons butter, at room temperature
7 tablespoons granulated sugar
2 large eggs
1 cup white chocolate chips

1½ cups dried blueberries
30 pecan halves

Preheat the oven to 350°F (175°C).

Oil 2 large cookie sheets. Melt the semi-sweet chocolate, then set aside to cool. Combine the flour, cocoa, cinnamon, baking powder, and salt. In a large bowl, cream the butter. Add the sugar and beat until light and fluffy. Add the eggs and beat until smooth. Stir in the melted chocolate. Add the dry ingredients and mix well. Fold in the white chocolate chips and blueberries.

Drop by tablespoons onto the prepared cookie sheets. Press a pecan half on top of each cookie. Bake until the cookies look dry and cracked but still feel soft when pressed lightly.

Remove from the oven and let stand on the sheet for 5 minutes.

Remove to a rack and let cool completely.

As a variation, you can drizzle melted white chocolate on top of the cookies after they're baked, instead of using the pecan halves.

Jean Fremont & Georgina Seifert
jfremont@sfu.ca
contributor: The British Columbia
              Blueberry Council
www.worldexport.com/bcblue

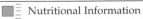

Nutritional Information

Per serving: Calories: 119,
Protein: 1 gm., Fat: 7 gm.,
Carbohydrates: 12 gm.

Blueberry Cheesecake
with Blueberry-Orange Compote

Yield: 24 servings

Blueberry filling:
4 cups blueberries, fresh or
    unthawed frozen
½ cup granulated sugar
¼ cup orange juice

Cheese filling:
2 pounds cream cheese
1 cup granulated sugar
4 large eggs

Crust:
1⅔ cups crumbled chocolate
    wafers (about 8 ounces of
    whole wafers)
3 tablespoons butter

Topping:
2 cups sour cream
⅓ cup granulated sugar
1 teaspoon vanilla

4 large oranges

Lightly butter a 9 or 10-inch springform pan. Preheat the oven to 350°F (175°C).

To make the blueberry filling, combine the blueberries, ½ cup sugar, and orange juice in a heavy medium saucepan. Bring to a boil over medium heat, stirring until the sugar dissolves. Reduce the heat and cook over low until the mixture thickens, stirring often. Remove from the heat and cool completely.

With an electric mixer, blend the cream cheese and 1 cup sugar well. Add the eggs one at a time, mixing well after each addition. Set aside.

Make the crust by melting the butter and adding to the wafer crumbs. Blend until moist crumbs form. Press into the bottom of the prepared pan. Spread the cheese filling over the crust. Spoon 1 cup of the blueberry filling on top of the cheese filling, and swirl with a small, pointed knife to marble. Reserve the remainder of the filling for the compote.

Place the cheesecake in the preheated oven, and bake until the filling is set, about 1 to 1¼ hours (use the longer time for the 9-inch pan). Remove from the oven and place on a rack. Prepare the topping by mixing the sour cream, ⅓ cup sugar, and vanilla. Gently

 Nutritional Information

Per serving: Calories: 313,
Protein: 5 gm., Fat: 21 gm.,
Carbohydrates: 26 gm.

but firmly press down the raised edges of the cheesecake, and spoon the topping evenly over the top. Bake for 5 more minutes. Transfer to a rack and cool.

Cover and refrigerate overnight.

Prepare the compote by peeling and segmenting the oranges. Using a small, sharp knife, cut between the membranes to remove the segments. Add the segments to the remainder of the blueberry filling.

To serve, remove the cheesecake from the pan, and transfer to a platter. Cut into slices, place them on plates, and spoon the blueberry -orange compote sauce over.

Jean Fremont & Georgina Seifert
jfremont@sfu.ca
contributor: The British Columbia
Blueberry Council
www.worldexport.com/bcblue

Index

141

Ask your local book or health food store to carry these titles, or you may order directly from:

Book Publishing Company
P.O. Box 99
Summertown, TN 38483

1-800-695-2241

Please add $2.50 per book for shipping and handling.

Vegetarian Resource Directory
  (includes a chapter on Internet resources)   . .$ 9.95

20 Minutes to Dinner 12.95
Almost No-Fat Cookbook 12.95
Delicious Jamaica! 11.95
Fabulous Beans 9.95
Foods That Cause You to Lose Weight 12.95
Lighten Up! with Louise Hagler 11.95
Natural Lunchbox 12.95
New Farm Vegetarian Cookbook 8.95
Nutritional Yeast Cookbook 9.95
Soyfoods Cookery 9.95
Table for Two 12.95
A Taste of Mexico 13.95
Tempeh Cookbook 10.95
Tofu Cookery 15.95
Tofu Quick & Easy 7.95
TVP© Cookbook 6.95
The Uncheese Cookbook 11.95

Table of Approximate Metric Equivalents	
1 teaspoon = 5 ml	1 cup = 230 ml
1 tablespoon = 15 ml	4 cups (1 quart) = .95 liter
¼ cup = 60 ml	1 ounce = 28 gm
⅓ cup = 80 ml	16 ounces = 30.5 cm
½ cup = 120 ml	